NUL
POINTS

THE UNOFFICIAL
EuroVision
QUIZ BOOK

First published in the UK in 2023 by Studio Press,
an imprint of Bonnier Books UK,
4th Floor, Victoria House, Bloomsbury Square, London, WC1B 4DA
Owned by Bonnier Books,
Sveavägen 56, Stockholm, Sweden

bonnierbooks.co.uk

13 5 7 9 10 8 6 4 2

All rights reserved
ISBN 978-1-80078-566-3

Written by Susie Rae
Edited by Jackie McCann
Designed by Maddox Philpot
Production by Giulia Caparrelli

A CIP catalogue record for this book is available from the
British Library

Printed and bound in Great Britain by Clays Ltd, Elcograf S.p.A.

NUL
POINTS

THE UNOFFICIAL
EUROVISION
QUIZ BOOK

STUDIO
PRESS

CONTENTS

INTRODUCTION

First held in 1956 with only a handful of competitors, the Eurovision Song Contest has grown over the past 70 years into the biggest, campest, wildest and most widely loved international singing contest in the world. These days, it's not even limited to Europe, with the weirdest and most wonderful talent from countries as far afield as Turkey, Australia and Canada flocking to compete. Whether you're batty about ballads, crazy for costumes, a sucker for a scandal, or just really into that massive hamster wheel, Eurovision has something for everybody.

But how big a fan are you really? This quiz book tests your knowledge of the highs and lows of Eurovision's reign as the world's most popular song contest (almost seven decades long and still counting!). Wrack your brains to remember the contest's wonderful winners and biggest losers, recall the most eye-catching costumes and baffling set pieces, and test your knowledge of Eurovision's fascinating history.

And above all else, try not to end up with "Nul Points"!

SPECIALIST SUBJECTS

Questions are divided into nine separate categories. Is your specialist subject past winners or record breakers? Perhaps you're more visual and it's the creative costumes, or the presenters that stand out for you? You may be a Eurovision history boffin, or perhaps you have a knack for recalling the scandals that almost derailed the performers and the show on the night? Whatever your specialist area, you'll find questions to suit you.

Here are your unoffical Eurovision categories. It's time to find out where your knowledge lies.

 Wonderful Winners

 Creating a Spectacle

 Chart Toppers

 Nul Points

 Presenters

 Eurovision History

 Record Breakers

 It's a Scandal

 Beyond Eurovision

1956 – 1959

THE EARLY YEARS

EUROVISION IS FOUNDED BY THE EUROPEAN BROADCASTING UNION • ELVIS PRESLEY HAS HIS FIRST NUMBER ONE IN THE UK • *A BEAR CALLED PADDINGTON*, BY MICHAEL BOND, IS PUBLISHED • THE FIRST MEETING OF THE EUROPEAN PARLIAMENTARY ASSEMBLY IS HELD IN STRASBOURG • PENCIL SKIRTS, CAPRI PANTS, AND BALLET PUMPS ARE ALL THE RAGE • THE EUROPEAN ECONOMIC COMMUNITY IS CREATED • LAUNCH OF SPUTNIK, THE WORLD'S FIRST SATELLITE • THE MINI MOTORCAR HITS THE STREETS OF THE UK • BRITAIN'S FIRST MOTORWAY OPENS • THE FIRST ELECTRIC GUITAR GOES ON SALE • BIRTH OF ROCK 'N' ROLL

1. Where was the first Eurovision Song Contest held?

2. Which country won the first Eurovision Song Contest in 1956?

3. Name all seven countries that competed in the first Eurovision Song Contest in 1956.

4. How many of the Founding Seven nations have won Eurovision at least once?

5. Which artist won the first Eurovision Song Contest?
   a Lys Assia
   b Corry Brokken
   c Freddy Quinn
   d Fud Leclerc

6. What was the winning song for the first Eurovision Song Contest?
   a 'Ne Crois Pas' (Don't Believe)
   b 'De Vogels Van Holland' (The Birds of Holland)
   c 'Refrain'
   d 'Il Est Là' (He's There)

7. Which Italian music festival sparked the creation of the Eurovision Song Contest?

🎤 **8.** In what language was the winning song of the first Eurovision Song Contest sung?

   a English
   b German
   c Dutch
   d French

🎤 **9.** Which of the following was not a voting rule in 1956?

   a Voting was done in secret
   b Jury members could vote for their own country
   c Jury members could allocate two votes to the same country
   d Performers were allowed to vote

🎤 **10.** How many songs did each country submit for the first Eurovision Song Contest?

🎤 **11.** Who presented the first Eurovision Song Contest?

   a Lohengrin Filipello
   b Anaïd Iplicjian
   c Hannie Lips
   d Jacqueline Joubert

🎤 **12.** True or False: The first Eurovision Song Contest was only broadcast via radio.

13. Which country voted on behalf of Luxembourg in 1956?

a Denmark
b Switzerland
c Italy
d Sweden

14. Besides 'Refrain', what other song did Lys Assia sing in 1956?

15. Which country came second in 1956?

16. What scandalous act did participants Birthe Wilke and Gustav Winckler perform onstage in 1957?

a They got into a fist fight
b They flew the wrong flag
c They took their clothes off
d They kissed

17. The 1957 contest saw the longest song in Eurovision history. What was the song?

a 'Net Als Toen' (Just Like Then)
b 'Corde Della Mia Chitarra' (Strings of my Guitar)
c 'Wohin, Kleines Pony?' (Where, Little Pony?)
d 'La Belle Amour' (The Beautiful Love)

18. How long was the longest song in Eurovision history?
a 5 minutes and 9 seconds
b 9 minutes and 5 seconds
c 4 minutes and 39 seconds
d 6 minutes and 12 seconds

19. Birthe Wilke and Gustav Winckler performed Eurovision's first duet. Which country were they representing?
a Belgium
b Denmark
c Austria
d France

20. Which country received the lowest score in 1957?
a United Kingdom
b Austria
c Denmark
d Luxembourg

21. Who presented the 1957 Eurovision Song Contest?
a Katie Boyle
b Anaid Iplicjian
c Hannie Lips
d Jacqueline Joubert

22. What was the maximum number of people allowed on stage per performance in 1957?

23. True or False: The 1956 winning country hosted the 1957 contest.

24. 1957 Danish performer Birthe Wilke first gained popularity by covering which popular song?
  - **a** 'Que Sera Sera' (What Will Be, Will Be)
  - **b** 'Walkin' After Midnight'
  - **c** 'Misty'
  - **d** 'Paper Doll'

25. How many countries participated in the second Eurovision Song Contest, in 1957?
  - **a** 10
  - **b** 12
  - **c** 14
  - **d** 16

26. Which country won the 1957 contest?

27. Which artist won Eurovision in 1957?
  - **a** Corry Brokken
  - **b** Margot Hielscher
  - **c** Lys Assia
  - **d** Danièle Dupré

28. What was the winning song in 1957?
   a 'La Belle Amour' (The Beautiful Love)
   b 'All'
   c 'Straatdeuntje' (Street Tune)
   d 'Net Als Toen' (Just Like Then)

29. True or False: 1957 was the first year to feature a scoreboard.

30. How many songs were performed in English in 1957?

31. In what language were most songs sung in 1957?

32. 1957 entrant Corry Brokken gave up performing in the 1970s. What profession did she take up instead?
   a Teacher
   b Doctor
   c Lawyer
   d Mortician

33. Which 1957 entrant has a theme park named after them?
- **a** Lys Assia (Switzerland)
- **b** Bobbejaan Schoepen (Belgium)
- **c** Nunzio Gallo (Italy)
- **d** Corry Brokken (The Netherlands)

34. What name did 1957 Danish performer Gustav Winckler perform under when touring England?

35. 1957 Belgian performer Bobbejaan Schoepen is best known for singing in which language?

36. Which country joined the contest for the first time in 1958?

 37. Which country won the 1958 contest?
- **a** The Netherlands
- **b** United Kingdom
- **c** Denmark
- **d** France

38. What time limit was introduced for Eurovision songs from 1958?
- **a** 3 minutes
- **b** 4 minutes
- **c** 5 minutes
- **d** 6 minutes

39. Who presented Eurovision in 1958?
- **a** Hannie Lips
- **b** Katie Boyle
- **c** Josiane Shen
- **d** Jacqueline Joubert

40. How many Grammy awards did 1958 Italian performer Domenico Modugno win for his song 'Nel Blu Dipinto di Blu' ('Volare')?

41. Swedish performer Alice Babs, from the 1958 Eurovision, is known for her collaborations with which popular American musician?
- **a** Duke Ellington
- **b** Miles Davis
- **c** Bob Dylan
- **d** Frank Sinatra

42. How many times did Belgian singer Fud Leclerc compete in the contest?

a   Two
b   Three
c   Four
d   Five

43. Which artist won the 1958 contest?

a   André Claveau
b   Solange Berry
c   Corry Brokken
d   Margot Hielscher

44. What was the winning song in 1958?

a   'Heel de Wereld' (The Whole World)
b   'Dors, Mon Amour' (Sleep, My Love)
c   'Ma Petite Chatte' (My Little Sweetie)
d   'Giorgio'

45. In 1957, previous winner Corry Brokken came joint last, becoming a victim of the "Curse of Number Two", but what is that?

O **46.** How many victims of the Curse of Number Two have scored "nul points"?

a Three

b Five

c Seven

d Nine

47. Why did the UK withdraw from the 1958 concert?

a They had a disagreement with the French jury

b They'd done too badly the previous year

c They thought World War II was still ongoing

d It was too expensive

48. What career is 1958 German performer Margot Hielscher best known for?

a Television presenter

b Film director

c Actress

d Ballet dancer

49. Lys Assia sang Eurovision's first bilingual song in 1958, but what languages did she sing in?

50. How many times did inaugural winner Lys Assia perform in Eurovision?

51. Which body part featured on the 1958
contest logo?

  a Hands
  b Hearts
  c Lips
  d Eyes

52. Which 1958 Eurovision song went on to sell
22 million copies worldwide?

53. Which country was the first to win Eurovision
more than once?

54. How many times has the United Kingdom
come second in the contest?

  a 1
  b 16
  c 20
  d 32

55. Which country won Eurovision in 1959?

  a The Netherlands
  b France
  c Austria
  d UK

56. Which country has the longest
participation streak?

57. Which artist won Eurovision in 1959?

a Brita Borg

b Christa Williams

c Jacques Pills

d Teddy Scholten

 58. What was the winning song in 1959?

a 'Oui, Oui, Oui, Oui' (Yes, Yes, Yes, Yes)

b 'Een Beetje' (A Little Bit)

c 'Irgendwoher' (From Somewhere)

d 'Der K und K Kalypso aus Wien' (The K and K Calypso from Vienna)

 59. Which French city hosted the 1959 contest?

a Perpignan

b Cannes

c Lyon

d Marseille

 60. Which country entered the contest for the first time in 1959?

a Ireland

b Turkey

c Monaco

d Finland

61. Which country withdrew in 1959?
 a UK
 b Luxembourg
 c Netherlands
 d Sweden

62. Who was banned from the jury from 1959 onwards?
 a Previous performers
 b Politicians
 c Members of the public
 d Music experts

63. Pearl Carr, UK entrant in 1959, went on to star in which 1990 musical by Stephen Sondheim?
 a *Follies*
 b *Assassins*
 c *Company*
 d *A Funny Thing Happened on the Way to the Forum*

64. What was the relationship between 1959 UK performers Pearl Carr and Teddy Johnson?

65. Who hosted the 1959 contest?
  a   Hannie Lips
  b   Sylvia Peters
  c   Jacqueline Joubert
  d   Lohengrin Filipello

 66. What set piece featured in 1959 Dutch performer Teddy Scholten's act?

67. What relation was 1959 performer Jacques Pills to the 1960 winner?

68. What were the first names of the Kessler Twins, who represented Germany in the 1959 contest?

69. Which magazine are the Kessler Twins famous for posing for?

70. Who was the first artist to compete for two different countries at Eurovision?

THE 60s

IN THIS DECADE...

THE SIXTIES ARE IN FULL SWING • BBC TELEVISION CENTRE OPENS • BERLIN WALL GOES UP • THE FIRST JAMES BOND FILM – *DR NO* – HITS THE CINEMAS • ELVIS, THE BEATLES AND THE ROLLING STONES RISE TO FAME • 8-TRACK CASSETTES GO ON SALE • MARY QUANT CREATES THE MINI SKIRT • ENGLAND WINS THE WORLD CUP • BBC2 BROADCASTS FOR THE FIRST TIME • BBC RADIO ONE, TWO, THREE AND FOUR LAUNCHES • STUDENTS RIOTS IN PARIS • EUROVISION IS BROADCAST IN COLOUR FOR THE FIRST TIME • APOLLO 11 MISSION GOES TO THE MOON • WOODSTOCK MUSIC FESTIVAL TAKES PLACE IN THE USA

71. The 1960 contest was hosted by the previous year's runner-up. Which country hosted the contest?

72. Who presented the 1960 Eurovision Song Contest?
  a Hannie Lips
  b Katie Boyle
  c Jacqueline Joubert
  d Mireille Delannoy

73. What colour outfit seems to bring the most success to Eurovision winners?
  a Green
  b Red
  c Black
  d White

74. What size of group is most likely to win Eurovision?
  a Three
  b Four
  c Five
  d Six

75. Which country won Eurovision in 1960?
- a France
- b Belgium
- c Monaco
- d The Netherlands

 76. Which artist won Eurovision in 1960?
- a Fud Leclerc
- b Anita Traversi
- c Jacqueline Boyer
- d Rudi Carrell

 77. What was the winning song in 1960?
- a 'Tom Pillibi'
- b 'Cielo e Terra' (Heaven and Earth)
- c 'Voi Voi' (Hey Hey)
- d 'Mon Amour Pour Toi' (My Love for You)

 78. What was the relationship between 1960 UK entrant Bryan Johnson and the previous year's UK performer?

 79. What was the name of 1960 Dutch performer Rudi Carrell's successful television show?
- a *Tonight with Rudi Carrell*
- b *Sit Down with Rudi*
- c *The Rudi Carrell Show*
- d *Rudi Talks*

80. In 1960, Wyn Hoop sang 'Bonne Nuit Ma Chérie' in what language?

81. What was 1960 Italian performer Renato Rascel accused of?

82. 1961 was the first year to have two countries in last place, with only one point each. Which countries came last?

83. Which country won Eurovision in 1961?
   a   Luxembourg
   b   France
   c   Spain
   d   UK

84. Who was the first person to present the Eurovision Song Contest twice?

85. In what language was the 1961 winning song performed?
   a   French
   b   German
   c   Italian
   d   Danish

86. **Which artist won Eurovision in 1961?**
- **a** Bob Benny
- **b** Dario Campeotto
- **c** Jean-Claude Pascal
- **d** Jean-Paul Mauric

 87. **What was the winning song in 1961?**
- **a** 'April, April'
- **b** 'Nous les Amoureux' (We Who Are in Love)
- **c** 'Al Di Là' (Beyond)
- **d** 'Angelique'

 88. **Dutch performer Greetje Kauffeld, from 1961, went on to lecture at which university?**
- **a** Utrecht University
- **b** Leiden University
- **c** University of the Arts, Hilversum
- **d** Vrije Universiteit Amsterdam

🎤 **89.** **Which three countries joined Eurovision for the first time in 1961?**

90. Which country did artist Lill-Babs represent in 1961?

a Sweden
b Yugoslavia
c Belgium
d Germany

91. Which of these contests is not organised by the Eurovision Broadcasting Union?

a Eurovision Young Dancers
b Turkvision Song Contest
c Eurovision Choir
d Junior Eurovision

92. Which country won Eurovision in 1962?

a Germany
b France
c The Netherlands
d Switzerland

93. Which artist won Eurovision in 1962?

a Isabelle Aubret
b Lola Novaković
c Camillo Felgen
d Eleonore Schwarz

94. What was the winning song in 1962?
a   'Le Retour' (The Return)
b   'Petit Bonhomme' (Little Guy)
c   'Ton Nom' (Your Name)
d   'Un Premier Amour' (A First Love)

95. How many entries scored the dreaded nul points in 1962?

96. Who presented the 1962 Eurovision?
a   Katie Boyle
b   Jacqueline Joubert
c   Mireille Delannoy
d   Lotte Wæver

97. Which country, in 1963, originally announced the wrong results when announcing their points?

98. Which country won Eurovision in 1963?
a   Sweden
b   Finland
c   Switzerland
d   Denmark

99. How many times has French singer Isabelle Aubret competed in Eurovision?

100. Who presented the 1963 Eurovision?
- **a** Katie Boyle
- **b** Renata Mauro
- **c** Josiane Shen
- **d** Erica Vaal

 101. What was the name of the political party founded by 1963 UK performer Ronnie Carroll?
- **a** The Liberal Democrats
- **b** The Rainbow Alliance
- **c** The Monster Raving Loony Party
- **d** Artists for Freedom

 102. What is the nationality of 1963 French entry Esther Ofarim?
- **a** French
- **b** Swedish
- **c** South African
- **d** Israeli

103. After 1963, Monégasque singer Françoise Hardy collaborated with all but one of these artists. Which one?

   a Blur

   b Iggy Pop

   c Oasis

   d Malcolm McLaren

 104. Which artist won Eurovision in 1963?

   a Grethe and Jørgen Ingmann

   b Esther Ofarim

   c Monica Zetterlund

   d Anita Thallaug

105. What was the winning song in 1963?

   a 'Een Speeldoos' (A Musical Box)

   b 'T'en Vas Pas' (Don't Leave)

   c 'En Gång I Stockholm' (Once Upon a Time in Stockholm)

   d 'Dansevise' (Dance Ballad)

106. Name the first country to score nul points on a début.

107. Which country won Eurovision in 1964?
  a Spain
  b Italy
  c France
  d The Netherlands

 108. Which artist won Eurovsion in 1964?
  a Robert Cogoi
  b Los TNT
  c Lasse Mårtenson
  d Gigliola Cinquetti

 109. What was the winning song in 1964?
  a 'Non Ho l'Età' (I'm Not Old Enough)
  b 'Le Chant de Mallory' (Mallory's Song)
  c 'Près De Ma Rivière' (By My River)
  d 'Warum Nur Warum?' (Why, Only Why?)

0 **110.** How many entries scored nul points in 1964?
  a) Two
  b) Three
  c) Four
  d) Five

 111. What title was 1964 Dutch entry Anneke Grönloh awarded by her home country in 2000?

112. Which 1964 performer was so impressed with their Austrian opponent Udo Jürgens' song 'Warum Nur Warum?' that they decided to cover it in their native language?

   a   Anita Traversi (Switzerland)
   b   Matt Monro (UK)
   c   Anneke Grönloh (The Netherlands)
   d   Rachel (France)

113. What was the nationality of the artist Nora Nova, who represtented Germany in 1964?

114. Gigliola Cinquetti represented Italy in 1964, then later hosted Eurovision in which year?

   a   1975
   b   1987
   c   1991
   d   2003

115. Who presented the 1964 Eurovision Song Contest?

   a   Lotte Wæver
   b   Josiane Shen
   c   Erica Vaal
   d   Sandie Shaw

116. There is no known recording of the 1964 contest. What was found in the tape canister marked 'Eurovision 1964' in BBC storage?

117. How many times has Sweden come last in the competition?

118. What is the most common type of artist to win Eurovision?
  a   Female soloists
  b   Male soloists
  c   Male/female duos
  d   Groups

119. How many countries participated in the 10th anniversary of the Eurovision Song Contest in 1965?

120. Name the country that won Eurovision in 1965?

121. Which artist won in 1965?
  a   France Gall
  b   Vice Vukov
  c   Kirsti Sparboe
  d   Simone de Oliveira

122. What was the winning song in 1965?

   a 'Als Het Weer Lente Is?' (When Will Springtime Come Again?)

   b 'Poupée de Cire, Poupée de Son' (Wax Doll, Sound Doll)

   c 'Walking the Streets in the Rain'

   d 'I Belong'

123. Which famous French recording artist wrote the winning song of 1965?

   a Charles Aznavour

   b Charles Trenet

   c Serge Gainsbourg

   d Johnny Halliday

124. Which country made their Eurovision debut in 1965?

125. Who presented the 1965 Eurovision Song Contest?

   a Renata Mauro

   b Erica Vaal

   c Laurita Valenzuela

   d Moira Shearer

126. How many countries left empty-handed, with nul points in 1965?

127. In which year did 1965 Dutch performer Conny Vandenbos gain a star on the Rotterdam Walk of Fame?

a 1966
b 1994
c 2000
d 2012

128. What type of music did Swedish performer Ingvar Wixell eventually become best known for?

129. Which country can claim the most Eurovision wins?

a Ireland
b France
c The Netherlands
d Sweden

130. How many times has the country with the most wins won the contest?

131. Who was the first Black artist to perform in Eurovision?

132. Austria holds the record for the longest wait between victories. How long was the wait between their first and second wins?

133. Which country won Eurovision in 1966?

   a Ireland

   b Austria

   c Yugoslavia

   d Norway

 134. Which artist won Eurovision in 1966?

   a Dickie Rock

   b Udo Jürgens

   c Lill Lindfors and Svante Thuresson

   d Kenneth McKellar

 135. What was the winning song in 1966?

   a 'Nygammal Vals' (New Old Waltz)

   b 'Yo Soy Aquél' (I'm the One)

   c 'Fernando en Filippo' (Fernando and Filippo)

   d 'Merci, Chérie' (Thank You, Darling)

 136. Who presented the 1966 ESC?

   a Josiane Shen

   b Erika Vaal

   c Willy Dobbe

   d Helga Guitton

0 **137.** How many countries were awarded the dreaded nul points in 1966?

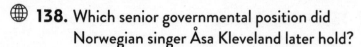 **138.** Which senior governmental position did Norwegian singer Åsa Kleveland later hold?

   a Minister of State
   b Minister of the Arts
   c Minister of Education
   d Minister of Culture

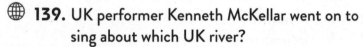 **139.** UK performer Kenneth McKellar went on to sing about which UK river?

   a River Clyde
   b River Thames
   c River Mersey
   d River Ouse

140. What was the most represented language (for songs) in the 1966 contest?

141. In what language was the 1966 winning song sung?

142. Which of these artists from the 1966 contest didn't go on to host Eurovision later?

   a Åse Kleveland
   b Kenneth McKellar
   c Lill Lindfors
   d Dickie Rock

143. How many male/female duos have
won Eurovision?

 144. What superstition did 1967 United Kingdom
performer Sandie Shaw start among
Eurovision artists?

 145. How many Eurovision songs have had only
a number for a title?

 146. Which country won Eurovision in 1967?
- **a** United Kingdom
- **b** Yugoslavia
- **c** Monaco
- **d** Spain

 147. Which artist scored a string of Number 1s
in the early 60s, then won Eurovision in 1967?
- **a** Eduardo Nascimento
- **b** Vicky Leandros
- **c** Sean Dunphy
- **d** Sandie Shaw

148. What was the winning song in 1967?
- **a** 'Puppet on a String'
- **b** 'If I Could Choose'
- **c** 'O Vento Mudou' (The Wind Changed)
- **d** 'Ring-Dinge-Ding'

149. Sandie Shaw encouraged an unknown artist to record 'It's Not Unusual', a song originally written for her. Name the artist.

a Englebert Humperdinck
b Elton John
c Cat Stevens
d Tom Jones

150. Which country went home with nul points in 1967?

a Sweden
b Switzerland
c Spain
d Swaziland

151. What career did Dutch performer Thérèse Steinmetz take up after she stopped singing?

a Dancer
b Painter
c TV presenter
d Sculptor

152. Eduardo Nascimento was the first Black man to perform in the Eurovision Song Contest. Which country did he represent in 1967?

a Italy
b Monaco
c Portugal
d Spain

153. Which country has hosted Eurovision more than any other?

154. What was notable about the way the 1968 contest was broadcast?

155. Which country won Eurovision in 1968?

a Spain
b Russia
c Yugoslavia
d Portugal

156. Which artist won Eurovision in 1968?

a Line & Willy
b Kristina Hautala
c Massiel
d Gianni Mascolo

157. Manuel Serrat should have represented Spain in 1968, but was replaced by Massiel before the contest. Why didn't Serrat perform?

158. What was the winning song in 1968?
a 'Guardando Il Sole' (Watching the Sun)
b 'Tausend Fenster' (A Thousand Windows)
c 'Jedan Dan' (One Day)
d 'La, La, La'

159. Rumour has it that Spanish dictator General Franco 'bought' votes and fixed the 1968 competition, robbing the bookmakers' favourite of the title. Who had been the favourite to win?

160. UK entry Cliff Richard had a hit with his song, reaching Number 1 in several countries. What was the name of the song?
a 'Motivations'
b 'Felicitations'
c 'Congratulations'
d 'Jubilations'

161. Who presented the 1968 Eurovision?
- **a** Katie Boyle
- **b** Laurita Valenzuela
- **c** Erica Vaal
- **d** Josiane Shen

162. Austria's 1968 entry Karel Gott later became known as The Golden Voice of which city?
- **a** Vienna
- **b** Budapest
- **c** Prague
- **a** Paris

163. 1969 saw the first tie-break situation in Eurovision history. How many countries tied for first place?

164. Name all the countries that won Eurovision in 1969.

165. How many times has Sweden won Eurovision?
- **a** Four
- **b** Five
- **c** Six
- **d** Seven

166. Who presented the 1969 Eurovision?
- **a** Valerie Singleton
- **b** Hannie Lips
- **c** Laurita Valenzuela
- **a** Willy Dobbe

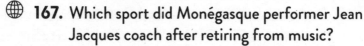

167. Which sport did Monégasque performer Jean Jacques coach after retiring from music?
- **a** Football (soccer)
- **b** Hockey
- **c** Tennis
- **d** Rugby

168. What career did Irish performer Muriel Day take up in the early 1970s?
- **a** Vocal coach
- **b** Laser therapist
- **c** Manicurist
- **d** Hypnotherapist

169. What did UK artist Lulu shout at the end of her 1969 performance to honour her Spanish hosts?

170. Where is Lulu from?

171. Two-time Eurovision entrant for Sweden, Tommy Körberg, later sang in the 10th anniversary concert of which successful musical?

172. In 1969, Swedish singer Siw Malmkvist became the first person in Eurovision to do what?
- **a** Perform from her home country via satellite link
- **b** Break an ankle on stage
- **c** Represent two different countries
- **d** Swear during her performance

173. Which Eurovision Song Contest has the shortest running time in Eurovision history?

174. What was the first country to win Eurovision on home ground?
- **a** Spain
- **b** UK
- **c** The Netherlands
- **d** France

175. Which of these songs was not a winning song in 1969?

a 'De Troubadour' (The Troubadour)

b 'Un Jour, Un Enfant' (One Day, One Child)

c 'Bonjour, Bonjour' (Hello, Hello)

d 'Boom Bang-a-Bang'

 176. Which of these artists did not win Eurovision in 1969?

a Salomé

b Muriel Day

c Lulu

d Lenny Kuhr

177. Who was the first woman to write a winning Eurovision song?

178. 1969 UK song 'Boom Bang-a-Bang' later became the theme tune for which sitcom?

a *Outnumbered*

b *Not Going Out*

c *Him and Her*

d *Cuckoo*

179. Which artist has had the most Eurovision wins?

180. How many people have written more than one winning Eurovision song?

181. Name the Eurovision song that has been covered the most.

THE 70s

IN THIS DECADE...

THE BEATLES BREAK UP • DENMARK, IRELAND AND THE UK JOIN THE EUROPEAN UNION • MICROSOFT AND APPLE ARE FOUNDED • BELL-BOTTOM TROUSERS, WIDE COLLARS AND PLATFORM SHOES ARE EVERYWHERE • FUNK, SOUL, DISCO AND PUNK ARRIVE ON THE MUSIC SCENE • PINK FLOYD AND LED ZEPELLIN ARE THE BIGGEST SELLING BANDS • THE WORLD POPULATION REACHES FOUR BILLION • LAUNCH OF THE FIRST SPACE SHUTTLE, THE *ENTERPRISE* • FIRST *STAR WARS* FILMS IS REALEASED • ELVIS PRESLEY DIES • *SPACE INVADER,* THE WORLD'S FIRST COMPUTER VIDEO GAME, HITS THE SHEVLES • SONY WALKMAN, THE FIRST PORTABLE AUDIO PLAYER, IS RELEASED • MARGARET THATCHER BECOMES THE UK'S FIRST FEMALE PRIME MINISTER

182. When was the 12-point voting system first introduced?

183. In which year was the Eurovision Song Contest the most watched programme in the UK?
a 1972
b 1973
c 1974
d 1975

184. Who presented Eurovision in 1970?
a Léon Zitrone
b Hughie Green
c Willy Dobbe
d Corry Brokken

185. Spanish entrant Julio Iglesias is uncle to popular singer Enrique Iglesias. True or false?

186. Luxembourg scored nul points for the first time in 1970. How many times have they received this score?

187. With multiple winners from the previous year, how was the host nation chosen for 1970?

a   Coin toss
b   Rock, paper, scissors
c   Pulling a name from a hat
d   A sing-off

188. What title was Belgian performer Jean Valée awarded in 1999?

a   Marquis
b   Baron
c   Knight
d   Jonkheer

189. What position did 1970 UK song entry 'Knock Knock, Who's There?' reach in the UK charts?

190. Which country hosted the 1970 Eurovision Song Contest?

191. Four countries boycotted the 1970 Eurovision Song Contest, but for what reason?

192. Who sang UK song entry, 'Knock Knock, Who's There?' in 1970?

a Barry Hopkins
b Sally Bobkins
c Mary Hopkin
d Poppy Copkin

193. Which country won Eurovision in 1970?

a United Kingdom
b Ireland
c France
d Germany

194. Which artist won Eurovision in 1970?

a Dana
b Guy Bonnet
c Hearts of Soul
d Jean Vallée

195. What was the title of the 1970 winning song?

a 'Waterman'
b 'Je Suis Tombé Du Ciel' (I Fell From Heaven)
c 'Marlène'
d 'All Kinds of Everything'

196. Dana later did which of the following:
- **a** Became President of Ireland
- **b** Served as a Member of the European Parliament
- **c** Became Lady Mayor of Belfast
- **d** Participated in the 1976 Montreal Olympics

197. How many times has the UK won Eurovison?
- **a** Four
- **b** Five
- **c** Six
- **d** Seven

198. Following the four-way tie in 1969, what rule was agreed in 1970 in the case of a tie-break situation?

199. Which country made its Eurovision debut in 1971?

200. What was allowed for the first time in 1971?

201. Who presented Eurovision in 1971?
- **a** Eamonn Andrews
- **b** Bernadette Ní Ghallchóir
- **c** Sinéad O'Connor
- **d** Cynthia Ní Mhurchú

202. Clodagh Rodgers created a stir in 1971 when she represented the UK in Dublin. What happened as a result?

a She went into hiding

b Eurovision was cancelled

c Her performance was interrupted

d She received threats from the IRA

203. What song did Clodagh Rodgers sing?

204. Which country won Eurovision in 1971?

a Malta

b Greece

c Monaco

d United Kingdom

205. Which artist won Eurovision in 1971?

a Joe Grech

b Karina

c Clodagh Rodgers

d Séverine

206. What was the winning song in 1971?

a 'Un Banc, Un Arbre, Une Rue' (A Bench, a Tree, a Street)

b 'Diese Welt' (This World)

c 'Vita Vidder' (White Horizons)

d 'Pomme, Pomme, Pomme' (Apple, Apple, Apple)

207. How many times did Swiss trio Peter, Sue and Marc compete in Eurovision?

208. Which internationally renowned ballet dancer presented Eurovision in 1972?
a   Maggie Philbin
b   Margot Fonteyn
c   Moira Shearer
d   Darcey Bussell

209. Which UK city hosted the 1972 contest?
a   London
b   Edinburgh
c   Brighton
d   Cardiff

210. Which country won Eurovision in 1972?
a   Luxembourg
b   France
c   Italy
d   Ireland

211. How many contestants took part in the first edition of Eurovision Young Musicians?
a   6
b   18
c   27
d   36

212. Who won Eurovision in 1972?

a   The New Seekers
b   Helen & Joseph
c   Milestones
d   Vicky Leandros

 213. What was the name of the 1972 winning song?

a   'Musika I Ti' (Music and You)
b   'Comme on S'aime' (How We Love Each Other)
c   'Après Toi' (After You)
d   'Amanece'

 214. German contestant Mary Roos placed third in the ESC in 1972. In 1999, she released a German language cover of which song?

a   'Like a Virgin', by Madonna
b   'Believe', by Cher
c   'My Heart Will Go On', by Celine Dion
d   'Simply the Best', by Tina Turner

215. What was notable about Irish singer Sandie Jones's performance in 1972?

a   It contained a 90-second whistling solo
b   It criticised the British government
c   It was performed through the medium of ventriloquism
d   It was sung in the Irish language

216. British act The New Seekers formed following the break-up of The Seekers. Where were members of the original Seekers from?

217. Which two countries has Croatian singer Téréza Kesovija represented in Eurovision?
- **a** Yugoslavia and Croatia
- **b** Slovenia and Slovakia
- **c** Croatia and Serbia
- **d** Yugoslavia and Monaco

218. The 1972 interval act featured stock footage from a British event. What was the event?

219. Which country holds the record for coming last the most often?
- **a** United Kingdom
- **b** Serbia
- **c** Norway
- **d** Greece

220. How many times has the host country won Eurovision?

221. Due to heightened security, what were audience members at the 1973 contest warned not to do, for risk of being shot by security personnel?

222. Who presented the 1973 ESC?
   a Hughie Green
   b Angela Rippon
   c Denise Fabre
   d Helga Guitton

 223. Which country won Eurovision in 1973?
   a United Kingdom
   b Luxembourg
   c Monaco
   d Israel

 224. Name the artist who won Eurovision in 1973.
   a Marion Rung
   b Mocedades
   c Anne Marie David
   d Martine Clémenceau

 225. What was the title of the 1973 winning song?
   a 'Tu Te Reconnaîtras' (You Will Recognise Yourself)
   b 'Je Vais Me Marier, Marie' (I'm Going to get Married, Marie)
   c 'Eres Tú' (It's You)
   d 'It's Just a Game'

226. What is the English translation of the 1973 Spanish group, Mocedades?
  a Youths
  b Juveniles
  c Brats
  d Thieves

227. What was the first non-European country to compete in Eurovision?

228. Swedish group The Nova had to change their name as it was previously the name of a country competing in the ESC. What was The Nova's original name?
  a Finland
  b Monaco
  c Israel
  d Malta

229. Why did France withdraw from Eurovision in 1974?

230. Why did Italy not broadcast the 1974 Eurovision song contest, despite competing in it?

231. What is the 1974 Portuguese entry credited with doing?

232. Which country made its Eurovision début in 1974?

233. Who presented Eurovision in 1974?
a Angela Rippon
b Corry Brokken
c Karin Falck
d Katie Boyle

234. Olivia Newtwon John represented the UK in 1974. Name the famous musical that she later starred in.

235. What record does Norwegian singer Anne-Karine Strøm hold?
a Only artist to finish last more than once
b Sang the highest note in ESC history
c Sang more words per minute than any other Eurovision song
d Only artist to be arrested mid-song

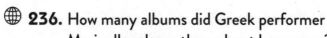 **236.** How many albums did Greek performer Marinella release throughout her career?
- **a** 50
- **b** 60
- **c** 70
- **d** 80

237. Which country won Eurovision in 1974?
- **a** Spain
- **b** Switzerland
- **c** Sweden
- **d** Ireland

238. Which artist won Eurovision in 1974?
- **a** Olivia Newton John
- **b** Mouth & MacNeal
- **c** Gigliola Cinquetti
- **d** ABBA

239. What was the title of the 1974 winning song?
- **a** 'Waterloo'
- **b** 'Long Live Love'
- **c** 'Si' (Yes)
- **d** 'Bye Bye I Love You'

240. The conductor for the 1974 Swedish entry, 'Waterloo', dressed up as which famous person?

241. Which musical is based on the songs of Eurovision superstars ABBA?

242. Which iconic British act performed in the interval in 1974?

243. What did 1974 presenter Katie Boyle do just before the contest started, due to a costume malfunction?

244. 1975 saw the second non-European country joining the contest. Name the country.

245. Why didn't Greece perform in 1975?

246. Which country won Eurovision in 1975?
- **a** The Netherlands
- **b** Italy
- **c** Norway
- **d** Turkey

247. Which artist won Eurovision in 1975?
- **a** The Swarbriggs
- **b** Nicole Rieu
- **c** Teach-In
- **d** Renato

248. What was the winning song in 1975?
- **a** 'That's What Friends are For'
- **b** 'Ein Lied Kann Eine Brücke Sein' (A Song May Be A Bridge)
- **c** 'Ding-a-Dong'
- **d** 'Toi' (You)

249. Who presented Eurovision in 1975?
- **a** Karin Falck
- **b** Leslie Judd
- **c** Yardena Arazi
- **d** Marlous Fluitsma

250. What major new system was introduced into Eurovision in 1975?

251. What was the relationship between the members of Irish Eurovision act, The Swarbriggs?

252. Which previous winner hosted Eurovision in 1976?

253. Why didn't Sweden participate in 1976?

254. Which country won the ESC in 1976?
  - **a** Ireland
  - **b** France
  - **c** United Kingdom
  - **d** Germany

 255. Which artist won Eurovision in 1976?
  - **a** Peter, Sue & Marc
  - **b** Brotherhood of Man
  - **c** Mariza Koch
  - **d** Chocolate Menta Mastik

 256. What was the winning song in 1976?
  - **a** 'Save Your Kisses for Me'
  - **b** 'Sing Sang Song'
  - **c** 'Mata Hari'
  - **d** 'We'll Live It'

 257. Who joined 1976 Swiss performers Peter, Sue & Marc on stage during their number?
  - **a** A clown
  - **b** A man in a hamster wheel
  - **c** A dancing nun
  - **d** A choir of children

258. Which language was most represented in the song entries of 1976?

259. Brotherhood of Man's 1976 entry, 'Save Your Kisses for Me' reached Number 1 in how many countries?

a   Four
b   Five
c   Six
d   Seven

260. The 1977 Eurovision Song Contest was postponed by a month. Why?

261. How many countries' entries were returning artists in 1977?

262. Who presented the ESC in 1977?

a   Katie Boyle
b   Angela Rippon
c   Jan Leeming
d   Bonnie Tyler

263. What does Austrian band Schmetterlinge's name translate as?

a   Butterflies
b   Ladybirds
c   Beetles
d   Blackbirds

264. Post Eurovision, Norwegian performer Anita Skorgan became famous for her voice work. Which of these films did she not lend her voice to?

   a *Anastasia*

   b *The Rescuers*

   c *Pocahontas*

   d *Quest for Camelot*

265. Which country won Eurovision in 1977?

   a Italy

   b Ireland

   c Norway

   d Spain

266. Which artist or artists won Eurovision in 1977?

   a Dream Express

   b Lynsey de Paul and Mike Moran

   c Heddy Lester

   d Marie Myriam

267. What was the winning song in 1977?

   a 'Rock Bottom'

   b 'Frère Jacques' (Brother James)

   c 'L'Oiseau et L'Enfant' (The Bird and the Child)

   d 'Mathima Solfege' (Dance Lesson)

268. What instruments did UK artists, Lynsey de Paul and Mike Moran both play in the 1977 ESC?

a   Electric guitars

b   Acoustic guitars

c   Grand pianos

d   Violins

269. Who is the longest-serving executive supervisor of Eurovision?

a   Clifford Brown

b   Frank Naef

c   Sarah Yuen

d   Christine Marchal-Ortiz

270. Despite not winning, Ireland's 1978 Eurovision entry became a successful musical theatre star. Can you name them?

271. Norwegian entry 'Mil Etter Mil' (Mile After Mile) scored nul points in 1978, but the song became a huge success in its home country. How many weeks did it spend at Number 1 in Norway?

272. Which country won Eurovision in 1978?

    a   Israel

    b   Greece

    c   Turkey

    d   Italy

 273. Which artist won Eurovision in 1978?

    a   Jahn Teigen

    b   José Vélez

    c   Baccara

    d   Izhar Cohen and Alpha Beta

274. What was the winning song in 1978?

    a   'A-Ba-Ni-Bi' (I Love You)

    b   'L'amour Ça Fait Chanter La Vie' (Love Makes Life Sing)

    c   'Bad Old Days'

    d   'Boom Boom'

275. What was notable about 1978's winning conductor Nurit Hirsh?

276. In which reality TV show did Israeli singer Izhar Cohen compete in 2020?

277. True or False: 1978 was the first year to have two presenters.

278. True or False: Léon Zitrone was the first male ESC presenter.

279. What was the original name of 1979 UK band Co-Co?
- **a** Mother's Pride
- **b** Daddy's Girls
- **c** Grandmother's Favourites
- **d** Co-Co-Co

280. The 1979 contest came down to a single point separating Spain from the eventual winner. Which country's votes tipped the scales?

281. How many countries participated in the 1979 Eurovision Song Contest?
- **a** 18
- **b** 19
- **c** 20
- **d** 21

282. What was notable about the location of the 1979 Eurovision Song Contest?

283. What was the response of some countries to the 1979 final being held in Jerusalem?

284. Which country won Eurovision in 1979?

   a Israel

   b Albania

   c Monaco

   d France

 285. Which act won Eurovision in 1979?

   a Gali Atari and Milk and Honey

   b Anne Marie David

   c Black Lace

   d Su Canción

 286. What was the winning song in 1979?

   a 'Heute in Jerusalem' (Today in Jerusalem)

   b 'Su Canción' (Your Song)

   c 'Sokrati' (Socrates)

   d 'Hallelujah'

287. What Eurovision record does 1979 Spanish entry 'Su Canción' hold?

   a The least amounts of words in a song

   b The most 'la's' in a song

   c The longest held note

   d The least popular song

288. In what language was the 1979 winning number sung?

289. Which historic figure joined the 1979 German entry onstage?

290. The United Kingdom's 1979 entry, Black Lace, are better known for which 1984 hit?

291. What is the biggest selling Eurovision single of all time?

292. Which year saw the introduction of the pre-song postcards, which introduced every country and artist?

  a 1970
  b 1971
  c 1972
  d 1973

293. In which two years, following their first introduction, were the pre-show postcards not used?

294. True or False: The pre-show postcards were first introduced to fill time due to the low number of entrants.

295. Which two countries has singer Elpida represented in the ESC, in 1979 and 1986?

296. Which two crimes were Swedish singer Ted Gärdestad falsely accused of?

297. The record for the largest gathering of ABBA impersonators is 368 people. In which city did this gathering take place?

298. How many countries has Dutch conductor Dolf van der Linde conducted for?

299. True or False: More English language songs have won Eurovision in total than all other languages put together.

THE 80s

IN THIS DECADE...

GREECE JOINS THE EU • MUSIC TELEVISION (MTV) REVOLUTIONISES POP MUSIC • PRINCESS DIANA AND PRINCE CHARLES MARRY • FIRST CD PLAYERS ARE SOLD IN JAPAN • MADONNA AND U2 ARE GLOBAL SUPERSTARS • SHOULDER PADS AND LEG WARMERS ARE IN • PRINCE WILLIAM IS BORN • MOTOROLA, THE FIRST MOBILE PHONE, ROLLS OUT COMMERCIALLY • THE YOUNG URBAN PROFESSIONAL, THE 'YUPPIE', IS BORN • SALLY RIDE IS THE FIRST WOMAN IN SPACE • HIP HOP, NEW WAVE AND HEAVY METAL ARE THE NEW MUSIC SOUNDS • *LIVE AID* IS WATCHED BY MORE THAN 1.9 BILLION PEOPLE GLOBALLY • *THE SIMPSONS* MAKE THEIR TV DEBUT • WORK BEGINS ON THE CHANNEL TUNNEL • SPAIN AND PORTUGAL JOIN THE EU • THE BERLIN WALL FALLS • *NINTENDO GAME BOY* IS RELEASED

300. In which city was the 1980 Silver Anniversary edition of the Eurovision Song Contest held?

301. What was the name of the 25th anniversary concert?

302. What was special about the 25th anniversary concert?
- **a** It was a fundraiser for the International Red Cross
- **b** It was not held in the 25th anniversary year
- **c** The host country was not a member of the European Broadcasting Union (EBU)
- **d** It was performed entirely by sock puppet

303. By the time of the 25th anniversary concert, how many Eurovision winners had there been?
- **a** 21
- **b** 25
- **c** 27
- **d** 29

304. How many previous Eurovision winners performed in the 25th anniversary concert?
- **a** Three
- **b** Four
- **c** Five
- **d** Six

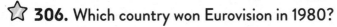 **305.** How many times has Morocco competed in Eurovision?

306. Which country won Eurovision in 1980?
- **a** France
- **b** Moldova
- **c** Ireland
- **d** United Kingdom

307. Which artist won Eurovision in 1980?
- **a** Prima Donna
- **b** Tomas Ledin
- **c** Télex
- **d** Johnny Logan

308. What was the winning song in 1980?
- **a** 'Just Nu!' (Right Now)
- **b** 'Love Enough for Two'
- **c** 'What's Another Year?'
- **d** 'Quédate Esta Noche' (Stay Tonight)

309. What were 1980 Luxembourg entry Sophie & Magaly's backing dancers dressed as?

310. How did 1980 presenter Marlous Fluitsma receive each country's votes?

311. Which artist has finished in the top three, on three separate occasions, without ever winning?

312. Which country's 1980 song was simply called 'Eurovision'?

313. What did 1981 Yugoslavian spokesperson Helga Vlahovic say when asked for her country's votes?

314. Previous winner Jean-Claude Pascal took 11th place in 1981. Which country did he represent?

315. Which country won Eurovision in 1981?
a United Kingdom
b Ireland
c Israel
d Switzerland

316. Which artist won Eurovision in 1981?
a Marty Brem
b Finn Kalvik
c Bucks Fizz
d Peter, Sue and Marc

317. What was the title of the 1981 winning song?

 a 'Horoscopes'
 b 'Feggari Kalokerino' (Summer Moon)
 c 'Io Senza Te' (Me Without You)
 d 'Making Your Mind Up'

318. Which country scored nul points in 1981?

319. What feature of Bucks Fizz's costumes caused a sharp intake of breath from the audience?

320. What incident ended the music career of Irish group Sheeba?

 a A plane crash
 b A car accident
 c A collision with a horse
 d Someone being mean on social media

321. UK band Bucks Fizz later changed their name to OBF. What does that stand for?

322. What career did Portuguese singer Carlos Paião pursue after his Eurovision performance in 1981?

 a Lawyer
 b Photographer
 c Doctor
 d Opera singer

323. Which country didn't compete in the 1982 contest, with their main broadcaster calling Eurovision "a monument to drivel"?

324. What question was asked in the opening act of the UK-hosted 1982 contest?

325. Who hosted Eurovision in 1982?
a   Jan Leeming
b   Michael Parkinson
c   Bruce Forsyth
d   Selina Scott

326. Which country won Eurovision in 1982?
a   Portugal
b   Norway
c   France
d   Malta

327. Name the artist that won the Eurovision Song Contest in 1982.
a   Nicole
b   Anna Vissi
c   Stella Maessen
d   Bardo

328. What was the title of the 1982 winning song?

   a 'One Step Further'

   b 'Él' (Him)

   c 'Ein Bisschen Frieden' (A Little Peace)

   d 'Hani?' (Where?)

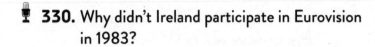 **329.** How many winning songs have been sung entirely in German?

 330. Why didn't Ireland participate in Eurovision in 1983?

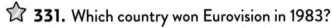 **331.** Which country won Eurovision in 1983?

   a Israel

   b Monaco

   c The Netherlands

   d Luxembourg

 332. Name the winning artist of Eurovision 1983.

   a Ofra Haza

   b Carola

   c Corinne Hermès

   d Danijel

333. What was the winning song in 1983?
- **a** 'Hi' (Alive)
- **b** 'Si La Vie est Cadeau' (If Life is a Gift)
- **c** 'Rendez-Vous' (Meeting)
- **d** 'Džuli' (Julie)

334. How many countries scored nul points in 1983?

335. British singer Carrie Gray went on to become a judge on what reality TV show?

336. Dutch singers Bernadette Kraakman and Ingrid Simons were members of which duo?
- **a** It Takes Two
- **b** Deux Points
- **c** Me and Der
- **d** Double Trouble

337. What was the relationship between German duo Hoffmann and Hoffmann?

338. Israel's Ofra Haza sang 'Hi', which became a hit in Europe and kickstarted Haza's career. Which 1998 animated film did Haza provide voice acting for?

🎤 **339.** Désirée Nosbusch, the presenter for the Luxembourg-hosted 1984 contest, was notable for being one of the youngest Eurovision presenters. How old was she?

🎤 **340.** How many languages did Désirée use when presenting the 1984 contest?

😲 **340.** Which country's artist was the first to be booed off the stage in 1984?

⭐ **342.** Name the country that won the ESC in 1984.
  a Finland
  b Sweden
  c Norway
  d Denmark

⭐ **343.** Which artist won Eurovision in 1984?
  a Herreys
  b Linda Martin
  c Dollie de Luxe
  d Rainy Day

⭐ **344.** What was the title of the 1984 winning song?
  a 'Diggiloo Diggiley'
  b 'Aufrecht Geh'n' (Stand Tall)
  c 'Terminal 3'
  d 'Avanti La Vie' (Go Forward in Life)

345. What did Ireland's entry sing about in their song 'Terminal 3'?

346. Which 1984 act was dubbed "the dancing deodorants" by a previous participant?

347. Which previous Eurovision contestant presented the contest in 1985?

348. What led the 1985 presenter to quip, "I just wanted to wake you up a little"?

349. In 1985, Germany were the favourites to win. Where did they finish?

350. True or False: In 1989, Germany's entry was so popular that bookmakers only offered odds against them winning.

351. Which country won Eurovision for the first time in 1985?
  a Germany
  b Yugoslavia
  c Norway
  d Sweden

352. Which artist won Eurovision in 1985?

   a Hot Eyes

   b Wind

   c Izhar Cohen

   d Bobbysocks!

353. What was the title of the winning song in 1985?

   a 'Für alle' (For Everyone)

   b 'Eläköön Elämä' (Long Live Life)

   c 'Love Is'

   d 'La Det Swinge' (Let it Swing)

354. How many singers were there in Norwegian act Bobbysocks!?

355. What genre of music did Turkish band MFÖ transition to in the years following their 1980s Eurovision performances?

356. What Eurovision record does German band Wind hold?

   a The only band to finish second twice

   b The only band with more than six members

   c The only band to finish in the top three four times without winning

   d The only band whose members are all under twenty

357. Why was the 1985 presenter "honestly happy" about the winning entry?

358. Which popular UK commentator gave their commentary from London, rather than attending the event in Sweden in 1985?

359. What was notable about Yugoslavia's 1985 selection, 'Pokora' by Josip Genda and Zorica Kondza?

360. Which two countries didn't attend the 1985 contest due to national days of mourning?

361. Which country made its Eurovision début in 1986?

362. Which country's entry performed the 500th song in Eurovision history, in 1986?
- **a** Luxembourg
- **b** Austria
- **c** Sweden
- **d** Portugal

363. In which popular 1997 film can you hear the voice of 1986 interval act Sissel Kyrkjebø?

364. Who is the youngest ever Eurovision winner?

365. Which previous Eurovision entrant hosted the 1986 contest, opening the night with a song called 'Welcome to Music'?

366. Which country won Eurovision in 1986?
a   France
b   Monaco
c   Belgium
d   Andorra

367. Name the winning artist of Eurovision 1986.
a   Sherissa Laurence
b   Sandra Kim
c   Daniele Simmons
d   Elpida

368. What was the title of the 1986 winning song?
a   'Pas Pour Moi' (Not For Me)
b   'Romeo'
c   'Yavo Yom' (A Day Will Come)
d   'J'aime La Vie' (I Love Life)

369. Which country holds the record for coming second the most?

370. How many times did Turkey make the top 10 in the 100% jury era?

371. Who was the first artist to win the Eurovision Song Contest twice?

372. The Soviet Union never competed in Eurovision, but how many former republics of the USSR have competed?

a 7
b 8
c 9
d 10

373. Which country won Eurovision in 1987?

a Ireland
b France
c Turkey
d Cyprus

374. Can you name the artist who won Eurovision in 1987?

a Wind
b Novi Fosili
c Johnny Logan
d Patricia Kraus

375. What was the title of the 1987 winning song?
- **a** 'Hold Me Now'
- **b** 'Laß die Sonne in dein Herz' (Let the Sun into Your Heart)
- **c** 'No Estás Solo' (You are not Alone)
- **d** 'Only the Light'

376. What was Tintin artist Hergé's contribution to the 1987 contest?

377. Students from which school presented flowers to the winning artist in 1987?

378. Which French singer presented the 1987 contest?
- **a** Johnny Halliday
- **b** Charles Aznavour
- **c** Julien Doré
- **d** Viktor Lazlo

379. Which country went home with the dreaded nul points in 1987?

380. Which famous duo did Israeli performers Datner & Kushnir impersonate during their 1987 performance?

381. Which city has played host to Eurovision the most often?

   a London, UK

   b Stockholm, Sweden

   c Dublin, Ireland

   d Amsterdam, The Netherlands

382. Why did Cyprus withdraw from the 1988 contest?

383. What was the opening act in the 1988 contest?

384. Which country won the ESC in 1988?

   a France

   b Austria

   c Luxembourg

   d Switzerland

385. Which artist won Eurovision in 1988?

   a Celine Dion

   b Scott Fitzgerald

   c Beathoven

   d Jump the Gun

386. What was the title of the winning song?

    a 'Go'

    b 'Staf I Ijus' (City of Light)

    c 'Ne Partez Pas Sans Moi' (Don't Leave Without Me)

    d 'Lisa, Mona Lisa'

387. How many points separated the first and second place artists in the 1988 contest?

388. What country is 1988 Swiss entrant Celine Dion originally from?

389. Celine Dion is the best-selling French-language recording artist of all time. At what age did Celine Dion begin her successful singing career?

390. What position in the UK charts did United Kingdom's 1988 entry 'If I Had Words' by Scottish singer Scott Fitzgerald reach?

    a Number 1

    b Number 2

    c Number 3

    d Number 4

391. What was the last French-language song to win Eurovision?

392. Which popular television show did 1988 director Declan Lowney go on to direct?

393. Lara Fabian, 1988 Belgian entry, gave her voice to the French version of which 1996 animated movie?

394. True or False: 1989 was the first year that the main acts did not include a returning artist?

395. What does the "count-back" tiebreaker rule state?

396. Which country scored nul points in 1989?

397. How many times did the artist performing in the final spot in the running order win Eurovision in the 1980s?

398. France's Nathalie Pâque and Israel's Gili Netanel were criticised in 1989 for being too young. How old were they?

399. What does OGAE stand for?

400. When was OGAE founded?

401. Which country won Eurovision in 1989?
- a Serbia
- b Norway
- c Yugoslavia
- d Greece

402. In what language was the winning song sung in 1989?

403. Name the winning artist of Eurovision 1989.
- a Riva
- b Live Report
- c Nathalie Pâque
- d Mariana Efstratiou

404. What was the title of the 1989 winning song?
- a 'Why Do I Always Get It Wrong?'
- b 'Nur ein Lied' (Just a Song)
- c 'La Dolce Vita' (The Sweet Life)
- d 'Rock Me'

405. Italy nearly didn't compete in 1989. Why not?

406. In which European city was the 1989 Eurovision Song Contest held?

407. Danish singer Birthe Kjær went on to write the song 'Hvor' vi fra?' in 2004 for which international event?

a   UEFA Euro Cup
b   Junior Eurovision Song Contest
c   Summer Olympics, Athens
d   Ryder Cup

408. What is the "Curse of 43"?

409. How many years have fallen victim to the Curse of 43?

D **410.** Of all the countries that have competed in Eurovision, how many have never won a contest?

411. True or False: Despite winning five times, no Luxembourger winner has actually been from Luxembourg.

THE 90s

IN THIS DECADE...

THE WORLD WIDE WEB IS BORN • HUBBLE SPACE TELESCOPE LAUNCHES • THE USSR BREAKS UP • EURO DISNEY OPENS IN FRANCE • THE EEC BECOMES THE EUROPEAN UNION • RIPPED JEANS, BOMBER JACKETS AND SCRUNCHIES ARE HIP AND TRENDY • THE CHANNEL TUNNEL OPENS TO TRAFFIC • *FRIENDS* IS A TV SENSATION • THE SPICE GIRLS AND OASIS ARE GLOBAL POP PHENOMENA • TAMAGOTCHI GO ON SALE • AUSTRIA, FINLAND AND SWEDEN JOIN THE EUROPEAN UNION • *HARRY POTTER AND THE PHILOSOPHER'S STONE* KICKS OFF THE BESTSELLING SERIES • THE BBC GOES ONLINE • *TITANIC* IS THE FIRST FILM TO TAKE MORE THAN $1 BILLION AT THE BOX-OFFICE • GOOGLE IS BORN • EASTERN EUROPEAN COUNTRIES TAKE PART IN EUROVISION FOR THE FIRST TIME

412. True or False: The 1989 winners attended the 1990 Eurovision Song Contest to present the trophy to their successors.

413. Which significant event of the late 80s was referenced in several songs in 1990?

414. What was the title of the 1990 opening act, referencing the host city of Zagreb?

415. What was notable about the ticket prices for the Yugoslavian-hosted 1990 contest?

416. Why did 1990 presenters Helga Vlahović and Oliver Mlakar nearly refuse to host the contest?

417. From 1990, an age limit was placed on artists performing in the contest. What is the youngest age allowed?

418. What was the name of the 1990 Eurovision mascot?

419. Who are the "Big Five" countries?

420. What benefit do the Big Five countries gain?

D 421. Which member of the Big Five has never scored nul points?

422. How many members of the Big Five were "Founding Seven" nations?

423. Which country won Eurovision in 1990?
- **a** France
- **b** Italy
- **c** Germany
- **d** United Kingdom

424. Which artist won Eurovision in 1990?
- **a** Joëlle Ursull
- **b** Emma
- **c** Toto Cutugno
- **d** Liam Reilly

425. What was the winning song in 1990?
- **a** 'Somewhere in Europe'
- **b** 'Insieme: 1992' (Together: 1992)
- **c** 'Som en Vind' (Like a Wind)
- **d** 'White and Black Blues'

426. What interrupted Spain's Azucar Moreno's number in 1990?

427. How many songs were sung in Swedish in 1990?

428. The 1991 contest was moved from Sen Remo to Rome due to security concerns surrounding which global event?

429. Which two countries tied for first place in 1991?
   a   Ireland and United Kingdom
   b   Greece and Denmark
   c   Sweden and France
   d   Switzerland and Cyprus

430. Which country ultimately won Eurovision in 1991?

431. Which country scored nul points in 1991?

432. Issues with which instrument interrupted the performance of the 1991 Luxembourg entry?

433. Issues with which instrument affected the 1991 Greek performance?
   a   Balalaika
   b   Guitar
   c   Saxophone
   d   Flute

434. What language did 1991 presenters Gigliola Cinquetti and Toto Cutugno speak primarily, for most of the ESC?

a English
b French
c Italian
d Spanish

435. Norwegian band Just 4 Fun claimed they performed poorly in the 1991 ESC due to focusing largely on what?

a Perfecting their look
b Coming up with their name
c Partying in Rome
d Doing press interviews

436. What was the relationship between Israeli performers Duo Datz?

437. UK performer Samantha Womack (née Janus) is best known for playing Ronnie in which British soap opera?

438. Which artist won Eurovision in 1991?

a Amina Annabi
b Thomas Forstner
c Sergio Dalma
d Carola

439. What was the winning song in 1991?

    a 'Le Dernier Qui a Parlé' (The Last One Who Spoke)

    b 'Mrs. Thompson'

    c 'Geef Het Op' (Give It Up)

    d 'Fångad av en Stormvind' (Captured by a Storm Wind)

440. Which city hosted the 1992 Eurovision Song Contest?

441. Which country competed for the last time in 1992?

 442. What was the name of the 1992 Eurovision mascot?

443. Which country won Eurovision in 1992?

    a Yugoslavia

    b Sweden

    c Germany

    d Ireland

444. Who was the winning artist in 1992?

    a Michael Ball

    b Linda Martin

    c Mia Martini

    d Wind

445. Name the winning song from 1992?

   a 'Why Me?'

   b 'Träume Sind Füe Alle Da' (Dreams Are There for Everyone)

   c 'Yamma Yamma'

   d 'One Step Out of Time'

446. What did Greek singer Cleopatra Pantazi become following her 1992 ESC performance?

   a A dentist

   b A nun

   c An airline pilot

   d A prison warden

447. Which previous winner wrote the 1992 winning song?

448. 1992 UK entry Michael Ball later performed in well-known musicals. Which one of these has he not performed in?

   a *Wicked*

   b *Les Misérables*

   c *Hairspray*

   d *Chitty Chitty Bang Bang*

 449. What was 1992 opening act (and 1991 winner) Carola seen doing during the voting section of the 1992 contest?

450. After retiring from music, Serbian performer Extra Nena gained a PhD in which subject?

a Performing arts

b Economics

c Literature

d Child psychology

451. What instrument did 1992 host conductor Anders Berglund play for the Yugoslavian entry?

452. Who presented the Ireland-based 1993 contest?

a Fionnuala Sweeney

b Val Doonican

c Ryan Turbridy

d Mary Kennedy

453. What is the smallest town to host the contest?

454. Which three former Yugoslav republics performed as independent countries for the first time in 1993?

455. What Eurovision rule was introduced for the first time in 1993?

456. 1993 was a close finish, but which country delivered the final deciding points?

457. Which two previous Eurovision winners performed in the 1993 interval?

458. Though six countries were relegated in 1993, only five of those did not perform in the following year's contest, as Italy withdrew. Which country was saved from relegation by Italy's withdrawal?

459. Which country won Eurovision in 1993?
- **a** Israel
- **b** Italy
- **c** Ireland
- **d** Iceland

460. Which artist won Eurovision in 1993?
- **a** Andrea Corr
- **b** Enya
- **c** Niamh Kavanagh
- **d** Mary Black

461. What was the winning song in 1993?
- a 'Better the Devil You Know'
- b 'In Your Eyes'
- c 'Hombres' (Men)
- d 'A Cidade' (A City)

462. How many countries have won the contest twice in a row?

463. True or False: Ireland has reached the top 5 a staggering 17 times.

464. True or False: The 1993 winner had the lowest winning score of any contest so far.

465. True or False: The 1993 winner became the biggest-selling single in its home country that year.

466. Which two countries appeared in the top three in both 1992 and 1993?

467. Which Celtic myth was retold in the 1993 opening ceremony?
- a Fionn Mac Cumhaill
- b Children of Lír
- c Eochaid and Étain
- d Diarmuid and Gráinne

468. Singer Barbara Dex has gone down in Eurovision history for her unflattering costume. Which country did she represent in 1993?

469. How many countries made their Eurovision début in 1994?

470. How many countries have won Eurovision three times in a row?

471. What successful dance performance was the interval act in 1994?

472. What successful dance duo were the leads in the 1994 interval performance?
   a   Ginger Rogers and Fred Astaire
   b   John Travolta and Olivia Newton-John
   c   Jean Butler and Michael Flatley
   d   Jennifer Grey and Patrick Swayze

473. Which country won Eurovision in 1994?
   a   Ireland
   b   Finland
   c   Sweden
   d   Cyprus

474. Which artist won Eurovision in 1994?

   a Paul Harrington and Charlie McGettigan

   b Edyta Górniak

   c Nina Morato

   d Marie Bergman and Roger Pontare

475. What was the winning song in 1994?

   a 'Rock 'n' Roll Kids'

   b 'Bye Bye Baby'

   c 'Waar is de Zon?' (Where is the Sun?)

   d 'Je Suis un Vrai Garçon' (I'm a Real Boy)

476. Which country didn't participate for the first time in 1994, due to relegation?

477. What performance from Eurovision 1994 was the biggest commercial success?

 478. In what language was the winning Eurovision song of 1994 sung?

   a French

   b English

   c Irish

   d German

0 479. Which country scored nul points in 1994?

480. Who presented the 1995 Eurovision Song Contest?

 a Gerry Ryan

 b Mary Kennedy

 c Graham Norton

 d Linda Martin

481. Rumours claimed that Ireland chose a deliberately bad song in 1995 to avoid hosting the contest again. This inspired an episode of what popular TV show?

482. True or False: 1995 was the last year in which none of the top three songs were sung in English.

483. With the risk of relegation leading to more countries missing a year, what was the last country to have a perfect attendance record?

484. Which Eurovision legend did the audience sing 'Happy Birthday' to in 1995?

485. Which country won Eurovision in 1995?

 a Ireland

 b Kosovo

 c Norway

 d Poland

486. Which artist won Eurovision in 1995?
   a   Stone & Stone
   b   Anabel Conde
   c   Love City Groove
   d   Secret Garden

 487. What was the winning song in 1995?
   a   'Nocturne'
   b   'Verliebt in Dich' (In Love with You)
   c   'Il Me Donne Rendez-Vous' (He Makes a Date With Me)
   d   'Núna' (Now)

488. Rolf Løvland, who represented Norway in 1995 as one half of duo Secret Garden, is perhaps best known for writing which chart-topping song?
   a   'Like a Prayer'
   b   'You Raise Me Up'
   c   'Hot Stuff'
   d   'Barbie Girl'

489. 1996 co-presenter Morten Harket was the frontman of which popular band?

490. Who represented the UK in 1996 with the song, 'Ooh Ahh, Just a Little Bit?'

491. 'Ooh Ahh, Just a Little Bit' featured in season one of which successful sitcom?

  a *Father Ted*
  b *Derry Girls*
  c *The IT Crowd*
  d *Absolutely Fabulous*

492. Which form of movement does 1995 Israeli entrant Liora now teach?

  a Ballet
  b Kick-boxing
  c Zumba
  d Yoga

493. In which reality TV show did Morten Harket participate in 2021?

494. True or False: 1996 was the first year to introduce televoting.

495. Which 1996 entrant also won a Grammy nomination for their song?

496. Which country entered Eurovision for the first time in 1996?

497. How many countries were unlucky enough to score nul points in 1996?

D 498. 1996 was the first year with a pre-qualifier round. How many countries were eliminated in this round?

☆ **499.** Which country won the 1996 Eurovision pre-qualifier round?

☆ **500.** Can you name the winning artist of the 1996 pre-qualifier round?

a   One More Time

b   Kathy Leander

c   Eimear Quinn

d   Leon

☆ **501.** What was the winning song in the 1996 pre-qualifier round?

a   'The Voice'

b   'Den Vilda' (The Wild Won)

c   'Ooh Aah, Just a Little Bit'

d   'Samo Ti' (Only You)

☆ **502.** Which country won the 1996 final?

a   Ireland

b   Cyprus

c   Sweden

d   Italy

503 Which artist won the 1996 final?
a One More Time
b Kathy Leander
c Eimear Quinn
d Leon

 504. Name the title of the winning song of Eurovision 1996.

505. Which rule was Estonian singer Maarja-Liis Ilus allowed to break in 1996?

506. Which language did French group L'Héritage de Celtes use for the first time in Eurovision history in 1996?
a Breton
b Occitan
c Provençal
d Elvish

 507. For which head of state did Irish singer Eimear Quinn perform in 2011?

508. Portuguese singer Lúcia Moniz is recognisable for her role in which romantic comedy?

a   *Bridget Jones's Diary*
b   *Love Actually*
c   *Notting Hill*
d   *Crazy, Stupid, Love*

509. True or False: 1996 was the last year where every country used instruments on stage.

510. Who was the first female Executive Supervisor for Eurovision?

511. In honour of the popular TV show *Father Ted*, what was the name given to the 1996 Eurovision Song Contest logo?

512. In 1996, the UK's Gina G had a worldwide hit with her song, but what place did she finish in the contest?

513. 1997 co-presenter Ronan Keating was a member of which popular band?

514. Katrina and the Waves represented the UK in 1997. What single are they best known for?

515. Which country does Katrina, of Katrina and the Waves fame, come from?

516. Singer Tor Endresen represented Norway in 1997. Later, he narrowly missed out on the opportunity to write a theme song for which film franchise?

a *Transformers*
b *The Marvel Cinematic Universe*
c *James Bond*
d *Star Wars*

517. Ireland came in second in 1997, but only received one douze points score – from which country?

518. True or False: Following the success of the previous year, the 1997 Eurovision Song Contest included a pre-qualifying round.

519. How many countries used televoting in 1997?

520. Why did Israel withdraw from the 1997 contest?

521. Which country was saved from relegation by Israel's voluntary withdrawal in 1997?

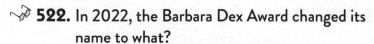

522. In 2022, the Barbara Dex Award changed its name to what?

  a You're a Vision award
  b Vision of Loveliness award
  c Night Vision award
  d Vision-on award

523. Which Dutch website presented the Barbara Dex Award until 2016?

524. Which artist won the first Barbara Dex Award, in 1997?

525. Which two countries went home with nul points in 1997?

526. Which four countries opted to use playback entirely, instead of on-stage instruments, in 1997?

527. Which country won Eurovision in 1997?

  a Croatia
  b North Macedonia
  c United Kingdom
  d Greece

528. What was the winning song in 1997?

   a 'Love Shine a Light'

   b 'Goodbye'

   c 'Zeit' (Time)

   d 'Probudi Me' (Awaken Me)

 529. Which charity was the 1997 winning number dedicated to?

 530. What kind of charity did Bosnian singer Alma Čardžić open following her 1997 ESC performance?

 531. 1997 French entrant Fanny released an album in 2009 covering the songs of which singer?

   a Eva Fitzgerald

   b Aretha Franklin

   c Edith Piaf

   d Nina Simone

532. Which Eurovision 'first' did Icelandic singer Paul Oscar achieve in 1997?

   a First use of the Icelandic language

   b First openly gay performer

   c First swear word in a Eurovision song

   d First person to earn negative points

533. Which country was 1998 co-presenter Terry Wogan from?

534. Which country is 1998 co-presenter Ulrika Jonsson originally from?

535. In which British city was the 1998 Eurovision Song Contest held?
   a   London
   b   Glasgow
   c   Birmingham
   d   Manchester

536. Which country scored nul points in 1998?

537. What dangerous act did Germany's Guildo Horn perform in 1998?

538. In 1998, Spain had to correct a mistake made with their points system after the contest. What was the mistake?

539. What faux pas did presenter Ulrika Jonsson make in 1998?

540. True or False: 1998 was the last contest to feature an orchestra.

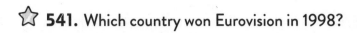

☆ **541.** Which country won Eurovision in 1998?

☆ **542.** Name the artist that won Eurovision in 1998.
- **a** Guildo Horn
- **b** Chiara
- **c** Dawn Martin
- **d** Dana International

☆ **543** What was the title of the 1998 winning song?
- **a** 'Où Aller?' (Where to Go?)
- **b** 'Diva'
- **c** 'Is Always Over Now?'
- **d** 'Nah Bogovi Slišijo' (Let the Gods Hear)

◉ **544.** Which previous Eurovision winner recorded the highest annual earnings for a female pop star in 1998?

🐁 **545.** What was prominently featured on the dress worn by Dana International during her 1998 reprise?

🌐 **546.** To which Pixar film did Estonian singer Koit Toome lend his voice for the Estonian dub?
- **a** *Brave*
- **b** *Toy Story 3*
- **c** *Cars*
- **d** *The Incredibles*

547 Who was the first transgender performer in Eurovision history?

548. True or False: 1999 was the first year without a presenter for Eurovision.

549. The 1999 contest ended with a rendition of previous winning song 'Hallelujah' as a tribute to the victims of which recent event?

550. What symbols decorated the stage for the 1999 contest?

551. Why did Croatian artist Marija Magdalena have points deducted in 1999?

552. What was the 800th song performed at Eurovision?

553. Which country won Eurovision in 1999?
- **a** Lithuania
- **b** Serbia
- **c** Sweden
- **d** Cyprus

554 Name the winning artist of Eurovision 1999.

a   The Mullans
b   Bobbie Singer
c   Times Three
d   Charlotte Nilsson

 555 What was the title of the 1999 winning song?

a   'All Out of Luck'
b   'Take Me to Your Heaven'
c   'Tha 'ne Erotas' (It Will Be Love)
d   'Believe 'n Peace'

 556. Who won the Barbara Dex Award that year?

557. In which city was the 1999 contest held?

558. Which of these countries did not perform in 1999?

a   North Macedonia
b   Denmark
c   Germany
d   Austria

559. How many times has Swedish performer Charlotte Perrelli (née Nilsson) competed in Eurovision?

560. True or False: The previous Israeli winners refused to attend the 1999 contest.

561. Which rule surrounding song content was abolished in 1999?

562. Which song holds the Eurovision record for the fewest lyrics?

563 What is the job of a stand-in?

564. Which Eurovision winner holds the record for most cumulative weeks spent on the UK albums' chart?

565 When did Ireland last win Eurovision?

566 True or False: Live animals have appeared on the Eurovision stage four times.

567 How many Eurovision winners have performed barefoot?

THE 00s

IN THIS DECADE...

NOKIA 1100 BECOMES THE BEST-SELLING PHONE OF ALL TIME • THE IPOD AND IPHONE ARE RELEASED • THE EURO BECOMES THE MAIN CURRENCY IN EUROPE • *THE DA VINCI CODE* IS A PUBLISHING SENSATION • *SPIRIT*, THE FIRST ROVER, LANDS ON MARS • EUROVISION SEMI-FINALS ARE INTRODUCED • CYPRUS, MALTA, CZECHIA, ESTONIA, HUNGARY, SLOVENIA, LITHUANIA, POLAND, SLOVKIA AND LATVIA JOIN THE EUROPEAN UNION • MUSIC SHARING TAKES OFF ON ITUNES AND *YOUTUBE* • *MYSPACE* BECOMES A SOCIAL MEDIA SENSATION • EVERYONE IS WEARING LOW-RISE JEANS, VELVET TRACKSUITS AND HEELYS • THE *X FACTOR* CHANGES THE FACE OF POP MUSIC • EMINEM AND BRITNEY SPEARS DOMINATE THE CHARTS • BULGARIA AND ROMANIA JOIN THE EU • BARACK OBAMA IS ELECTED THE 44TH PRESIDENT OF THE USA

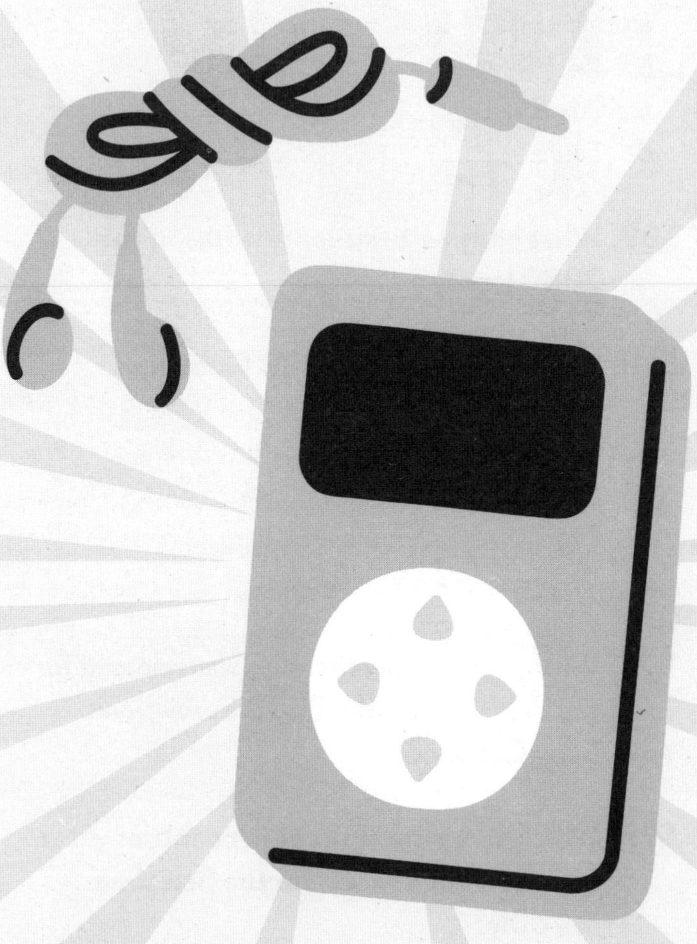

568. Which country made their Eurovision debut in 2000?

  a Lithuania
  b Liechtenstein
  c Luxembourg
  d Latvia

569. What body part was represented in the 2000 logo?

570. What award did the 2000 Eurovision logo win?

  a Design Week award
  b UK Graphic award
  c Excellent Swedish Design award
  d Creativity of Europe award

571. What piece of merchandise was released for the first time for the 2000 Eurovision Song Contest?

572. Which three non-European countries broadcast the contest for the first time in 2000?

573. What was the strange title of the interval act in 2000?
- **a** Let's Take a Boat Ride Down the Danube
- **b** When the Rain Falls in Zaragoza
- **c** Once Upon a Time, Europe Was Covered with Ice
- **d** A Strange Thing Happened on the Way to Athens

 574 Which country's 2000 act involved a plea for peace in the form of a same-sex kiss?

 575. What popular Eurovision catchphrase was coined in 2000?

😮 **576.** True or False: The 2000 winners were ultimately disqualified for using a vocoder.

☆ **577.** Which country won Eurovision in 2000?
- **a** Switzerland
- **b** Ukraine
- **c** Denmark
- **d** Finland

578. Name the winning artist or artists of Eurovision 2000.

    a Olsen Brothers

    b Nathalie Sorce

    c Claudette Pace

    d XXL

 579. What was the winning song in 2000?

    a 'Millennium of Love'

    b 'When Spirits are Calling My Name'

    c 'La Vita Cos'è' (What is Life?)

    d 'Fly on the Wings of Love'

580. True or False: The 2000 winner was a surprise, with bookmakers offering low odds of their victory.

581. Which artist won the Barbara Dex Award in 2000?

582. Israeli band PingPong caused controversy in their home country by doing what during their 2000 performance?

583. With the language rule lifted the previous year, how many of the 24 Eurovision songs were sung, at least partially, in English?

130

584. Denmark hosted the 2001 contest. How long had it been since they'd last hosted?

585. True or False: The 2001 venue was the smallest Eurovision venue in over a decade.

586. Who presented the 2001 contest?

587. The 2001 winner had several Eurovision "firsts". Which of these was *not* one of their firsts?

  a The first former USSR republic to win
  b The youngest winner in the history of the ESC
  c The oldest winner in the history of the ESC
  d The first black winner

588. How many times has a Eurovision song been performed in a made-up language?

589. True or False: The previous year's winners returned to perform in the interval act in 2001.

590. Name the Polish artist who won the Barbara Dex Award in 2001.

591. Which country won Eurovision in 2001?

    a   North Macedonia

    b   Slovenia

    c   Estonia

    d   Bosnia and Herzegovina

 592. Which artist won Eurovision, 2001?

    a   Gary O'Shaughnessy

    b   SKAMP

    c   Lindsay Dracass

    d   Tanel Padar, Dave Benton & 2XL

 593. Can you name the winning song from 2001?

    a   'Everybody'

    b   'No Dream Impossible'

    c   'Strings of My Heart'

    d   'Sevgiliye Son'

594. True or False: The host nation took last place in 2002.

595. Which non-relegated country withdrew in 2002?

596. Which country was saved from relegation by another country's withdrawal in 2002?

597. What was the theme of the 2002 contest?

598. 2002 presenters Annely Peebo and Marko Matvere performed a number during the interval. What was it called?

  a   'Music is the Story of My Life'
  b   'Sing Me a Story'
  c   'A Little Story in the Music'
  d   'A Lot of Music in the Story'

599. What voting system was brought back to the contest in 2002?

600. Why was the voting system changed in 2002?

601. Which artist, representing Greece, won the Barbara Dex Award in 2002?

602. Which two countries received their only relegations in 2002?

603. Which country won Eurovision in 2002?

604. Can you name the 2002 winning artist?

  a   Manuel Ortega
  b   Marie N
  c   Prime Minister
  d   Karolina

605. What colour was the show-stopping dress worn by the 2002 winner?

606. What was the winning song in 2002?
- **a** 'I Wanna'
- **b** 'I Can't Live Without Music'
- **c** 'Tell Me Why'
- **d** 'Il Faut du Temps' (It Takes Time)

607. Which two countries tied for third place in 2002?

608. In 2002, how many of the 24 songs didn't include any English language lyrics?

609. True or False: The 2002 winning song was a huge hit in its home country.

610. Which country scored nul points in 2003?

611. What reason did UK act Jemini give for their out-of-tune singing during their 2003 performance?

612. Which country competed in Eurovision for the first time in 2003?

613. 2003 saw the highest number of participants in Eurovision history. How many countries participated?

614. Which Latvian city hosted the 2003 contest?

615. What was the theme of the 2003 contest?
a Magical Moonlight
b Magical Rendez-vous
c Dancing in the Moonlight
d Voulez-vous Couchez Avec Moi, Ce Soir?

616. What was the slogan for the 2003 contest?

617. What did commentator Terry Wogan say was to blame for the UK's poor score in 2003?

618. Which of these countries did not use a jury to vote in 2003?
a Ireland
b UK
c Russia
d Bosnia and Herzegovina

619. What was the first English-language song to be awarded the dreaded nul points?

620. True or False: 2003 was the first contest in over 10 years with entirely new performances.

621. Which country won Eurovision in 2003?
  a   Israel
  b   Turkey
  c   Malta
  d   United Kingdom

622. Name the winning artist of 2003.
  a   Sertab Erener
  b   t.A.T.u
  c   Esther Hart
  d   Louisa Baileche

623. What was the title of the 2003 winning song?
  a   'Ne Ver', Ne Boysia' (Don't Believe, Don't Fear)
  b   'Everyway That I Can'
  c   'Let's Get Happy'
  d   'Ne Brini' (Don't Worry)

624. Which 2003 entrants were dubbed "the bad girls of pop" due to their scandalous behaviour?

625. The artist t.A.T.u won the Barbara Dex Award in 2003. Which country did they represent?

626. In 2003 a song was sung in an imaginary language for the first time. Which country did the singer represent?

627. True or False: 2003 had the biggest gap between first and third place in Eurovision history.

628. What was the theme of the 2004 contest?
   a Under the Same Roof
   b Over the Rainbow Together
   c Under the Same Umbrella
   d Under the Same Sky

629. Which four countries made their Eurovision debut in 2004?

630. What replaced the relegation rule in 2004?

631. How many times has a country received nul points in a semi-final?

632. Which four non-competing countries broadcast the 2004 contest?

633. What piece of merchandise was released shortly after the 2004 contest for the first time?

O **634.** Which of these countries received nul points in the 2004 semi-final?
- **a** France
- **b** Norway
- **c** Greece
- **d** Switzerland

O **635.** How many countries received nul points in the 2004 Eurovision final?

636. Which three countries automatically qualified for the final in 2004, without competing in the semi-final?

637. Which country won the 2004 semi-final?
- **a** Bosnia and Herzegovina
- **b** Turkey
- **c** Ireland
- **d** Serbia and Montenegro

638. Which artist won the 2004 semi-final?
- **a** Ivan Mikulić
- **b** Toše Proeski
- **c** Željko Joksimović
- **d** Re-Union

639. Name the winning song from the 2004 semi-final.
- **a** 'Lane Moje' (My Sweetheart)
- **b** 'Neiokõsõ' (Path)
- **c** 'In the Disco'
- **d** 'The Image of You'

640. Four languages were heard at Eurovision for the first time in 2004. What were they?

641. Name the Romanian recipient of the Barbara Dex Award in 2004?

642. Which country won the Eurovision final in 2004?
- **a** Russia
- **b** Poland
- **c** France
- **d** Ukraine

643. True or False: It was the winning country's first time competing in Eurovision.

644. Which artist won the Eurovision final in 2004?
- **a** Sakis Rouvas
- **b** James Fox
- **c** Julia Savicheva
- **d** Ruslana

645. What was the winning song in the 2004 Eurovision final?
- **a** 'Believe Me'
- **b** 'You are the Only One'
- **c** 'Wild Dances'
- **d** 'I Admit'

646. Which previous winner's "Last Video" was played as part of the 2004 interval act?

647. Which two countries made their Eurovision debut in 2005?

648. In *Parting of the Ways*, the epic season finale of 2005's *Doctor Who* season, what Eurovision-inspired insult did the Doctor use against the Daleks?

649. The UK's 2005 entry, Javine, beat which well-known British model in the national heats?

650. Which Eurovision entrant from the 1970s became the best-selling Latin artist worldwide?

651. What was the theme of the 2005 contest?
a   Awakening
b   Becoming
c   Dawning
d   Yawning

652 True or False: The 2005 contest saw the return of the live orchestra.

653. Which participating countries did not televote in either round for the 2005 contest?

654. In 2005, a new rule was introduced regarding voting. What was it?

655. Which country won the 2005 semi-final?

656. Which artist won the semi-final in 2005?
a   Suntribe
b   Glennis Grace
c   Marian van de Wal
d   Luminita Anghel and Sistem

657. Which song won the 2005 semi-final?
- **a** 'Let Me Try'
- **b** 'Make My Day'
- **c** 'Love Me Tonight'
- **d** 'Cool Vibes'

658. Which country's 2005 act featured yodelling, a Eurovision first?

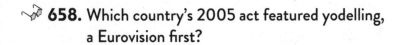

659. Which country won Eurovision, 2005?
- **a** The Netherlands
- **b** Greece
- **c** Germany
- **d** Portugal

660. Which artist won the 2005 Eurovision final?
- **a** NOX
- **b** Martin Vučić
- **c** Vanilla Ninja
- **d** Helena Paparizou

661 What was the title of the winning song in the 2005 Eurovision final?
- **a** 'Nobody Hurt No One'
- **b** 'My Number One'
- **c** 'The War is Not Over'
- **d** 'Ela Ela' (Come Baby)

662. True or False: The 2005 winner was the only automatically qualified song outside of the Big Four to win the contest.

663. Which country hosted *Congratulations: 50 Years of the Eurovision Song Contest*?

664. *Congratulations: 50 years of the Eurovision Song Contest* was named after which Eurovision entry?

665. How many votes were cast in *Congratulations*?
- **a** 1 million
- **b** 2.5 million
- **c** 3.6 million
- **d** 5.2 million

666. Who presented *Congratulations: 50 years of the Eurovision Song Contest*?

667. How many songs were entered into *Congratulations*?

668. Which song was ranked as the greatest song of the first 50 years of Eurovision at the *Congratulations* event in 2005?

669. Which of these songs did not reach the top five in the *Congratulations* event?
- **a** 'Hold Me Now' by Johnny Logan
- **b** 'Save Your Kisses for Me' by Brotherhood of Man
- **c** 'My Number One' by Helena Paparizou
- **d** 'Congratulations' by Cliff Richard

670. Which country provided the interval act for the *Congratulations* event?

671. The *Congratulations* interval act included a singer from which popular boyband?

672. 2006 was the first year where each country didn't read out all their votes. Why was this?

673. Who presented the 2006 contest?

674. On which ancient symbol was the logo for Eurovision 2006 based?
- **a** The Gordian Knot
- **b** The Celtic Cross
- **c** The Phaistos Disc
- **d** The Egyptian Ankh

675. What was the theme of the 2006 contest?

   a   Feel the Beat

   b   Feel the Heat

   c   Feel the Groove

   d   Feel the Rhythm

676. What did 2006 Dutch spokesperson Paul de Leeuw pretend to give the presenter during the voting announcements?

677. Which country made their Eurovision debut in 2006?

678. Which country did not compete in the 2006 contest due to a voting scandal in their national final?

679. In 2006, the 1000th Eurovision song was performed. By which country?

680. Which country won the 2006 semi-final?

681. Which artist won the 2006 semi-final?

   a   Hari Mata Hari

   b   Lordi

   c   Dima Bilan

   d   Carola Häggkvist

682. What was the winning song for the 2006 semi-final?
- **a** 'Show Me Your Love'
- **b** 'Never Let you Go'
- **c** 'Hard Rock Hallelujah'
- **d** 'La Coco-Dance'

683. How many points did last-place entry Malta gain in 2006?

684. What did the 2006 Lithuanian act, LT United, declare themselves in their song?

685. The artist Nonstop won the Barbara Dex Award in 2006. Which country did they represent?

686. Which country won the 2006 final?
- **a** Finland
- **b** Denmark
- **c** Norway
- **d** Sweden

687. What iconic piece of costume are the 2006 winning artists never seen without?

688. What hit song are the 2006 Spanish entry Las Ketchup best known for?

689. What was the theme of the 2007 contest?
- **a** True Fantasy
- **b** Fantasy Island
- **c** True Love
- **d** Love is an Island

690. How many countries competed overall in the 2007 contest?

691. Which four countries made their Eurovision debut in 2007?

692. Which country didn't compete in 2007 due to a series of poor results?

693. Who presented the award to the winning entry in 2007?

694. In 2007, a new rule was introduced when setting the running order. What was the rule?

695. True or False: In 2007, all of those allowed to choose their place in the running order chose spots in the first half of the evening.

696. Name the country that won the Eurovision semi-final in 2007.

697. Which artist won the semi-final in 2007?

   a   Kabát

   b   Marija Šerifović

   c   Frederik Ndoci

   d   The Jet Set

 698. Which song won the 2007 semi-final?

   a   'Time to Party'

   b   'Malá Dáma' (Little Lady)

   c   'Molitva' (Prayer)

   d   'Vertigo'

 699. Who designed the costumes for 2007 Austrian act Eric Papilaya?

700. What four languages featured in the 2007 Ukrainian song, 'Dancing Lasha Tumbai'?

701. What did Verka Serduchka claim the title of his song, 'Dancing Lasha Tumbai' meant?

 702. What symbol did 2007 Ukrainian entry Verka Serduchka wear on his head during his performance?

   a   The Ukrainian flag

   b   A sickle

   c   A heart

   d   A star

703. What 2015 comedy film included a cameo from 2007 Ukrainian entry Verka Serduchka?

704. What colour is associated with Verka Serduchka?

705. What type of creature did 2007 Swiss entry DJ BoBo claim to be?

706. What were 2007 UK entry Scooch dressed as?

707. Which country won the 2007 final?
  a Montenegro
  b North Macedonia
  c Serbia
  d Ireland

708. Which artist won the 2007 final?
  a Marija Šerifović
  b Verka Serduchka
  c 4Fun
  d Roger Cicero

709. Name the winning song from the 2007 final?
  a 'Molitva' (Prayer)
  b 'Song Number 1'
  c 'Flying the Flag'
  d 'Yassou Maria' (Hello Maria)

710 In what language was the 2007 winning song sung?

711 In which city did Eurovision 2007 take place?

712. What girl group joined 2007 Serbian entry Marija Šerifović onstage?

713. Despite being largely unpopular, the 2007 United Kingdom entry, 'Flying the Flag (For You)' was awarded douze points from Malta. Why?

714. How many rounds were there in the 2008 contest?

715. In 2008, French singer Sébastien Tellier caused controversy within his home country for his refusal to do what?

716. What did Sébastien Tellier drive onstage during his 2008 number, 'Divine'?
   a   An electric car
   b   A go-kart
   c   A golf buggy
   d   A scooter

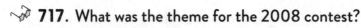

717. What was the theme for the 2008 contest?

   a Wall of Sound

   b Waves of Sound

   c Confluence of Sound

   d Sound and Vision

718. Which 1979 song by The Buggles was performed as part of the opening act for the first 2008 semi-final?

719. Which two nations had their Eurovision debut in 2008?

720 Which five countries automatically qualified for the 2008 final?

721 Which country won the first semi-final in 2008?

   a Norway

   b Armenia

   c Greece

   d The Netherlands

722. Which artist won the first semi-final in 2008?

   a Isis Gee

   b Nico & Vlad

   c Dima Bilan

   d Kalomira

723. What was the winning song for the first semi-final in 2008?
a 'Qélé, Qélé' (Let's Go, Let's Go)
b 'Secret Combination'
c 'For Life'
d 'Your Heart Belongs to Me'

724. What were the 2008 Latvian performers dressed as?

725. How did 2008 French entry Sébastien Tellier hit the high notes?

726. Since 2008, what has the Eurovision Grand Prix resembled?

727. In 2008, Spanish entrant Rodolfo Chikilicuatre began his song playing what instrument?

728. Which country won the second semi-final in 2008?
a Denmark
b Portugal
c Ukraine
d Croatia

729. Which artist won the second semi-final in 2008?

a   Ani Lorak
b   Olta Boka
c   Paolo Meneguzzi
d   Charlotte Perelli

 730. What was the winning song for the second semi-final in 2008?

a   'Hero'
b   'Zemrën e Lamë Peng' (Hearts Trapped in Time)
c   'Shady Lady'
d   'Wolves of the Sea'

 731. Which unconventional entry represented Ireland in 2008?

 732. Which iconic Irish act did the 2008 entry apologise for?

733. Andorran artist Gisela won the Barbara Dex Award in 2008. What did she wear?

a   A bronze and silver metallic tutu
b   The national costume of Andorra
c   A full-length pink négligée
d   A back plastic, hooded robe

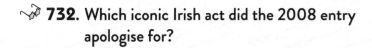

153

734. The 2008 Ukrainian entry first applied to represent her country in Eurovision in which year?

735. Estonia's 2008 act held up signs with pictures of which vegetable?

736. Andorran entry Gisela later provided the Catalan and Spanish singing voices for which Disney character?

737. How did the Azerbaijani artists Elnur & Samir dress for their 2008 performance?

738. What did Bosnia and Herzegovina's 2008 performer Pokušaj emerge from?
  a   A giant cake
  b   A bunch of sunflowers
  c   A washing basket
  d   A rubbish bin

739. Which country's high-energy 2008 performance included dancers dressed as Roman soldiers, pyrotechnics and giant gears as part of the set?

740. Which country won the 2008 final?

   a   Greece

   b   Russia

   c   Azerbaijan

   d   Spain

 741. Which artist won the 2008 final?

   a   Gisela

   b   Andry Abraham

   c   Ani Lorak

   d   Dima Bilan

 742. What was the title of the winning song?

   a   'Believe'

   b   'Shady Lady'

   c   'All Night Long'

   d   'Baila el Chiki-Chiki' (Dance the Chiki-Chiki)

 743. Which Disney character did 2008 Russian entry Dima Bilan provide the Russian voice for?

   a   Baloo in *The Jungle Book*

   b   Prince Hans in *Frozen*

   c   Aladdin

   d   WALL-E

744. Dima Bilan, the 2008 Russian entry, previously competed in Eurovision in which year?

745. Why did Georgia withdraw from the 2009 contest?

746. Swedish performer Malena Ernman is the mother of which famous activist?

747. Which mythological creature was seen in the logo for the 2009 contest?
  a   Firebird
  b   Phoenix
  c   Dragon
  d   Unicorn

748. Which non-European country sent their own commentators to Eurovision in 2009, despite not competing?

749. Which popular commentator resigned their position following the result of the 2008 contest, saying that the voting was strategic and no longer based on the music?

750. Who took on the role of commentator for the BBC in 2009?

0 **751.** Which country earned nul points in the first 2009 semi-final?

752. Which country won the first semi-final in 2009?

753. Which artist won the first semi-final in 2009?
   a   Waldo's People
   b   Inga & Anush
   c   Elena Gheorghe
   d   Yohanna

754. What was the title of the winning song for the first semi-final that year?
   a   'The Balkan Girls'
   b   'Jan Jan' (My Dear)
   c   'What If We'
   d   'Is It True?'

755. What prevented the Spanish public from participating in the 2009 semi-final televote?

756. Which country won the second semi-final in 2009?
   a   Greece
   b   Norway
   c   Azerbaijan
   d   Estonia

757. Which artist won the second semi-final in 2009?

   a AySel & Arash

   b Alexander Rybak

   c Igor Cukrov ft. Andrea Šušnjara

   d Sasha Son

758. Which American model joined German act Alex Swings Oscar Sings! onstage in 2009?

759 Zoli Ádok of Hungary won the Barbara Dex Award in 2009, for wearing what?

   a Ripped jeans

   b Plastic jeans

   c Red jeans

   d Green jeans

760. What instrument did the 2009 Norwegian entry Alexander Rybak play onstage?

761. Where was Alexander Rybak born?

762. True or False: 'Fairytale' the song for Norway, was the first non-UK entry to reach top ten in the UK charts since 1987.

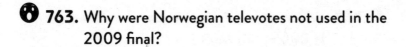

763. Why were Norwegian televotes not used in the 2009 final?

764. Which country won the 2009 final?
- **a** Norway
- **b** Italy
- **c** Israel
- **d** Malta

765. Which artist won the 2009 final?
- **a** Alexander Rybak
- **b** Waldo's People
- **c** Chiara
- **d** Jade Ewen

766. What was the title of the winning song in the 2009 final?
- **a** 'Be My Valentine (Anti Crisis Girl)'
- **b** 'It's My Time'
- **c** 'Miss Kiss Kiss Bang'
- **d** 'Fairytale'

767. Which successful composer wrote the 2009 UK entry 'It's My Time'?

   a Tim Rice

   b Elton John

   c Andrew Lloyd Webber

   d Gary Barlow

768 The 2009 UK entry was chosen in a reality TV show. What was the show called?

769. How many of the 25 songs in the 2009 final were at least partially sung in English?

770. In 2009, Ukrainian act Svetlana Loboda was accompanied on stage by back-up dancers dressed as what?

   a Celtic warriors

   b Vikings

   c Roman soldiers

   d Spartans

771. Alexander Rybank's smash hit of 2009 appeared on his début album. What was the title of the album?

772. In what year was the generic Eurovision logo introduced?

773. Which country has suffered the longest streak without a win?

a Norway

b Belgium

c Portugal

d Italy

774. What is the longest period of time a country has gone without winning?

775. Who is the oldest winner of Eurovision?

776. What nationality is fictional European Broadcasting Union (EBU) spokesperson Lynda Woodruff?

777. The first Opening Ceremony for Eurovision took place in 2009, in Moscow. Where was the ceremony held?

a In front of the Kremlin

b Olimpiysky Arena

c Lev Yashin Stadium

d Gorky Park

778. Where is the Eurovision in Concert pre-party usually held?

779. Which Eurovision winning number was performed with a group of 80,000 people, setting a World Record for karaoke singing? Was it...

a Lordi singing 'Hard Rock Hallelujah' in Helsinki's Market Square

b ABBA ripping up 'Waterloo' by Stockholm City Hall

c Bucks Fizz shaking their stuff to 'Making Your Mind Up' in Hyde Park, London

d Alexander Rybak performing 'Fairytale' outside the Oslo Opera House

780. When was the first Junior Eurovision Song Contest?

781. What was the venue for Eurovision 2009?

a State Kremlin Palace

b Moscow International House of Music (MMDM)

c Olympic Indoor Arena

d The Tchaikovsky Concert Hall

782 Which three non-participating countries broadcast the first JESC?

a Canada, Japan and South Africa

b Estonia, Finland and Germany

c Andorra, Bosnia and Herzegovina and Iceland

d Australia, USA and New Zealand

783. How old do you have to be to enter Junior Eurovision?

784. In the JESC, what language do songs mainly need to be sung in?
a The host country's language
b A made-up language
c The performer's language
d English

THE 10s

IN THIS DECADE...

DONALD TRUMP BECOMES US PRESIDENT • PRINCE WILLIAM MARRIES KATE MIDDLETON • EVERYONE IS USING INSTAGRAM AND POSTING SELFIES • EUROVISION ENTERS THE *GUINNESS BOOK OF RECORDS* AS THE WORLD'S LONGEST RUNNING ANNUAL SONG COMPETITION • SPOTIFY CHANGES THE FACE OF ONLINE MUSIC • ADELE, ED SHEERAN AND TAYLOR SWIFT DOMINATE THE CHARTS • THE ICE BUCKET CHALLENGE RAISES MORE THAN $2 MILLION FOR CHARITY • SKINNY JEANS AND CROP TOPS ARE IN • *POKÉMON GO* CAPTIVATES THE WORLD • YOUTUBERS ARE AMONG THE FIRST INFLUENCERS • THE EUROPEAN UNION WINS THE NOBEL PEACE PRIZE • CROATIA JOINS THE EU • PARIS AGREEMENT ON CLIMATE CHANGE IS ADOPTED • TIKTOK LAUNCHES • UK VOTES TO LEAVE THE EU • FIDGET SPINNERS TAKE OFF • THE COVID-19 PANDEMIC BEGINS

785. Which four countries withdrew from the 2010 contest?

786. What was the theme of the 2010 contest?
a   Share the Moment
b   Breaking Borders
c   Blue Skies
d   Hearts on Fire

787. Which country won the first semi-final in 2010?
a   Portugal
b   Iceland
c   Belgium
d   Greece

788. Which artist won the first semi-final in 2010?
a   Tom Dice
b   Filipa Azevedo
c   Aisha
d   Hera Björk

789. What was the name of the winning song for the first semi-final in 2010?
a   'OPA!'
b   'What For?'
c   'Ovo Je Balkan' (This is the Balkans)
d   'Me and My Guitar'

790. In 2010, how did Serbian contestant Milan Stanković distinguish himself?

791. True or False: 2010 was the first time Greece didn't qualify for the grand final.

792. In 2010, Norwegian broadcaster NRK decided, for cost reasons, not to broadcast another international event, in order to host Eurovision. What was the event?

793 Which country won the second semi-final in 2010?

a Turkey
b Ireland
c Israel
d Cyprus

794. Which artist won the second semi-final in 2010?

a Sofia Nizharadze
b MaNga
c Paula Seling & Ovi
d Safura

795. Can you name the winning song from the second semi-final in 2010?

    a 'We Could Be the Same'
    b 'Life Looks Better in Spring'
    c 'It's for You'
    d 'This Is My Life'

796. What colour was the "red carpet" in the 2010 opening ceremony?

797. The 2010 Moldovan entry 'Run Away' became an internet meme due to Sergey Stepanov's performance on which instrument?

798. What insects did Belarusian band 3+2 dress as during their 2010 performance?

799. Where did Moldovan viral sensation Sunstroke Project and Olia Tira finish in the 2010 final?

800. Which country won the 2010 final?

    a Greece
    b Turkey
    c Germany
    d Belgium

801. Which artist won the 2010 Eurovision final?
- **a** Jessy Matador
- **b** Paula Seling & Ovi
- **c** Alyosha
- **d** Lena Meyer-Landrut

 802. What was the winning song in 2010?
- **a** 'Satellite'
- **b** 'Playing With Fire'
- **c** 'It's All About You'
- **d** 'Run Away'

803. What instruments did Romanian act Paula Seling & OVI play during their 2010 number, 'Playing With Fire'?

804. How many studio albums has 2010 German entry Lena Meyer-Landryt released?

 805. What was the theme of the 2011 contest?
- **a** Dance to the Beat
- **b** Feel the Beat
- **c** Feel your Heart Beat
- **d** Love to Dance

806. Which German city hosted the 2011 contest?

807. True or False: 2011 was the fourth time that Germany hosted Eurovision since its reunification.

808. In 2011, the addition of which country turned the Big Four into the Big Five?

809. Who presented the 2011 contest?

810. The 2011 logo was based on a gesture made by the previous year's winner. What was it?

811. True or False: The 2010 winner attempted to defend their title in 2011.

812. Which country won the first semi-final in 2011?
  a Finland
  b Greece
  c Serbia
  d Malta

813. Which artist won the first semi-final in 2011?
  a Ell and Nikki
  b Kati Wolf
  c Loukas Giorkas ft. Stereo Mike
  d Magdalena Tul

814. What was the winning song in the first semi-final in 2011?

   a 'One More Day'
   b 'Watch My Dance'
   c 'Coming Home'
   d 'Da Da Dam'

815. Singer Eldrine, was crowned winner of the 2011 Barbara Dex Award. Which country did she represent?

816. What is the "Curse of Green"?

817. Who was the first victim of the Curse of Green?

818. What vehicle was ridden by one half of 2011's Moldovan act Zdob si Zdub?

819. Which country won the second semi-final in 2011?

   a Sweden
   b Austria
   c Estonia
   d The Netherlands

820. Which artist won the second semi-final in 2011?

   a 3JS
   b Poli Genova
   c Dana International
   d Eric Saade

821. What was the winning song of the second semi-final in 2011?

   a 'Ding Dong'
   b 'Love in Rewind'
   c 'Na Inat' (With Stubbornness)
   d 'Popular'

822. Italy returned to the contest in 2011 after a long absence. Where did they finish in the final?

823. True or False: 2011 was the first year to have more songs sung in French than English.

824. Which country won the 2011 final?

   a Greece
   b Sweden
   c Denmark
   d Azerbaijan

825. Which artist won the 2011 final?
- **a** Ell and Nikki
- **b** Raphael Gualazzi
- **c** Nina
- **d** Nadine Beiler

 826. What was the winning song in the 2011 final?
- **a** 'Running Scared'
- **b** 'I Can'
- **c** 'Angel'
- **d** 'One More Day'

827. Which reality TV show kick-started the career of 2011 Irish entry Jedward?

828. What is the relationship between the members of Jedward?

829. What was the title of Jedward's 2011 song?

830. True or False: 2011 Azerbaijan entrants Ell and Nikki didn't know each other before the contest.

831. What was the theme of the 2012 contest?
- **a** Light your fire!
- **b** Live the dream!
- **c** Set the world on fire!
- **d** Feel the music!

832. Which previous Eurovision winner co-presented the 2012 contest?

833. Which country won the first semi-final in 2012?
- **a** Denmark
- **b** Ireland
- **c** Russia
- **d** Cyprus

834 Which artist won the first semi-final in 2012?
- **a** Compact Disco
- **b** Mandinga
- **c** Buranovskiye Babushki
- **d** Valentina Monetta

835. What was the winning song in the first semi-final in 2012?
- **a** 'Should've Known Better'
- **b** 'Woki Mit Diem Popo' (Shake Your Bottom)
- **c** 'Sound of Our Hearts'
- **d** 'Party for Everybody'

836. How many times was 2012 Swedish entry 'Euphoria' certified platinum?

   a   8
   b   9
   c   10
   d   11

837. Why did Albania choose not to broadcast the 2012 semi-final?

838. Which of these languages was heard for the first time in the 2012 contest – Udmurt, Georgian or Azerbaijani?

839. How many returning acts performed in 2012?

840. Which country won the second semi-final in 2012?

   a   Serbia
   b   Portugal
   c   Norway
   d   Sweden

841. Which artist won the second semi-final in 2012?
- **a** Loreen
- **b** Anri Jokhadze
- **c** Maya Sar
- **d** Nina Badrić

842. What was the winning song in the second semi-final in 2012?
- **a** 'Don't Close Your Eyes'
- **b** 'Be My Guest'
- **c** 'Love Unlimited'
- **d** 'Euphoria'

843. Which other major international event caused Poland to withdraw in 2012?

844. Rona Nishliu of Albania won the Barbara Dex Award in 2012? What did she have curled around her neck during her performance?
- **a** A snake
- **b** A fox tail
- **c** A dreadlock
- **d** A feather boa

845. Which of these countries has never participated in Eurovision?

a Armenia

b Ukraine

c Estonia

d Liechtenstein

846. Which popular 1960s performer represented the UK in 2012?

847. What did Russian act Buranovskiye Babushki do on stage in 2012?

a Milk a cow

b Bake bread

c Spin yarn

d Churn butter

848. Which country won the 2012 final?

a Cyprus

b Sweden

c Switzerland

d Albania

849. Which artist won the 2012 final?

a Roman Lob

b Jedward

c Loreen

d Pasha Parfeny

850. What was the winning song in the 2012 final?
- **a** 'Should've Known Better'
- **b** 'Aphrodisiac'
- **c** 'Waterline'
- **d** 'Euphoria'

851. Who is the oldest participant in Eurovision history?
- **a** Switzerland's Emil Ramsauer
- **b** Croatia's 75 Cents
- **c** UK's Engelbert Humperdinck
- **d** Belgium's Sandra Kim

852. What was the theme of the 2013 contest?
- **a** We Are United
- **b** Reunited and It Feels So Good
- **c** We Are One
- **d** Stronger Together

853. What animal appeared on the 2013 logo?

854. What surprising item of clothing did Finnish singer Krista wear for her 2013 performance?
- **a** An astronaut's helmet
- **b** A wedding dress
- **c** A monk's robes
- **d** A policeman's uniform

855. Which Swedish city hosted the 2013 contest?

856. 1991 winner Carola Häggkvist performed during the 2013 interval act. What effect was prominently used in her performance?

  a Dry ice / smoke
  b Strobe lighting
  c Wind machine
  d A single spotlight

857. What position did 2013 Danish entry 'Only Teardrops' reach in the Danish charts after the contest?

858. What did Greece's 2013 act promise in their number?

859. Who presented Eurivision in 2013?

860. What is the name of Eytan Fox's 2013 Israeli comedy film celebrating Eurovision?

  a *Muffins*
  b *Pop tarts*
  c *Cupcakes*
  d *Donuts*

861. True or False: 2013 ESC featured the first solo presenter in Eurovision history.

862. Why did Turkey exit the contest in 2013?

863. How many of the Big Five countries reached the top ten in 2013?
a None
b One
c Three
d Five

864. What was unusual about Swedish contestant Euphoria's opening act for the first semi-final in 2013?

865. Which country won the first semi-final in 2013?
a Italy
b Denmark
c United Kingdom
d France

866. What happened to Aliona Moon, Moldovan entry's dress in 2013?
- **a** It lit up like the Moon
- **b** It lit up in flames
- **c** It lit up like a lighthouse
- **d** It went up like a balloon

867. Norway has finished bottom of the leaderboard how many times?

 868. How many Eurovision Song Contests were there before 2013?

869. In what year did Barbara Dex herself compete in Eurovision?

870. What colour was the dress worn by Barbara Dex when she inspired the eponymous award?
- **a** Green
- **b** Black
- **c** Beige
- **d** Pink

871. The 2013 Serbian artists, Moje 3, met on which reality TV show?

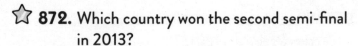

872. Which country won the second semi-final in 2013?

  a   Switzerland
  b   Hungary
  c   San Marino
  d   Azerbaijan

873. Which act won the second semi-final in 2013?

  a   Koz Mostra & Agathonas Iakovidis
  b   PeR
  c   Farid Mammadov
  d   Sophie & Nodi

874. How many countries participated in 2013?

875. What were 2013 Montenegro artists Who See dressed as during their performance?

876. Which 1980s pop star represented the UK in 2013?

  a   Kim Wilde
  b   Annie Lennox
  c   Bonnie Tyler
  d   Deniece Williams

877. Where did the UK representative for 2013 come from?

   a Scotland
   b England
   c Wales
   d Northern Ireland

878. When was the Eurovision Song Contest previously held in the 2013 host city?

879. Which country won the 2013 final?

   a Finland
   b Denmark
   c Azerbaijan
   d Serbia

880. Which artist won the 2013 final?

   a Emmelie de Forest
   b Farid Mammadov
   c Zlata Ognevich
   d Cascada

881. What was the winning song in the 2013 final?

   a 'Only Teardrops "
   b 'Hold Me'
   c 'Alcohol is Free'
   d 'Lonely Planet'

882. Which global dance sensation represented Germany in 2013?

883. Where did the German act finish in the 2013 final?

884. Where is 2013 Irish act Ryan Dolan originally from?

885. Which country took last place in the 2013 final?

886. What was the theme for the 2014 contest?
 a #FollowUs
 b #JoinUs
 c #CopyUs
 d #CopyCats

887. What role did long-time Eurovision fanatics Australia play in the 2014 contest?

888. What jewel featured on the 2014 logo?

889. What was each 2014 artist asked to create in a unique way for the postcards introducing each country?

890. Who presented Eurovision in 2014?

891. Which iconic number was celebrated by the 2014 contest hosts in a special musical segment?

892. Which of these popular Eurovision artists was not featured in the 2014 Museum of Eurovision History?

   a Lordi

   b Gina G

   c ABBA

   d Johnny Logan

893. Who won Most Claps in the 2014 Eurovision Book of Records?

894. Who won Highest Note in the 2014 Eurovision Book of Records?

895 How many years in a row did San Marino artist Valentina Monetta compete in Eurovision?

896. Which country won the first semi-final in 2014?

897. Which artist won the first semi-final in 2014?

    a   Sanna Nielsen

    b   Axel Hirsoux

    c   Tolmachevy Twins

    d   The Common Linnets

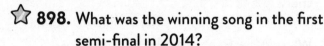 **898.** What was the winning song in the first semi-final in 2014?

    a   'Wild Soul'

    b   'Calm After the Storm'

    c   'Start a Fire'

    d   'Moj Svijet'

899. What did the 2014 Polish entry declare in their song?

900. Attention-seeker Valija Matačiūnaitė won the Barbara Dex Award in 2014? Which country did she represent?

901. What colourful combination did Valija Matačiūnaitė wear for her performance?

    a   Black and blue

    b   Blue and orange

    c   Orange and black

    d   Black and green

☆ **902.** How many countries took part in each of the semi-finals in 2014?

☆ **903.** Altogether there have been 66 Eurovision Song Contests, but how many winners have there been?

☆ **904.** What is the English translation of 'Wurst'?
   a Bacon
   b Sausage
   c Black pudding
   d White pudding

🎤 **905.** What is the English translation of Montenegro's 2014 song 'Moj Svijet'?

🎤 **906.** True or False: The UK came last in 2014.

🐕 **907.** What iconic prop was used in the 2014 Ukrainian number 'Tick-Tock'?

🐕 **908.** What colour did Austrian singer Conchita Wurst wear during her 2014 performance?
   a Red
   b Gold
   c Black
   d White

909. Which country won the 2014 final?
   a France
   b United Kingdom
   c Greece
   d Austria

 910. Which artist won the 2014 final?
   a Conchita Wurst
   b The Common Linnets
   c Sanna Nielsen
   d Softengine

⭐ **911. What was the winning song in the 2014 final?**
   a 'Calm After the Storm'
   b 'Hunter of Stars'
   c 'Rise Like a Phoenix'
   d 'Undo'

912. True or False: The 2014 contest holds the record for the highest number of countries in the grand final.

913. What is the greatest number of entries in a grand final in Eurovision history?

914. How many times had Swedish act Sanna Nielsen applied to represent her country before finally succeeding in 2014?

915. What is the real name of 2014 Austrian artist Conchita Wurst?

916. Conchita Wurst's name comes from the common German expression, "das ist mir doch alles Wurst". What does this mean?
- **a** "Pass the sausage"
- **b** "Pass the ketchup"
- **c** "I love frankfurters"
- **d** "It's all the same to me"

917. What was the theme for the 2015 contest?
- **a** Building Bridges
- **b** Bridge Over European Waters
- **c** Reaching For the Sky
- **d** The Sky's the Limit

918. Which country made its Eurovision debut in 2015?

919. Which two countries were awarded nul points in 2015?

920. Which two countries' similar album covers sparked accusations of plagiarism in 2015?

921. What sound from the audience was edited out from the 2015 contest?

922. True or False: Australia auto-qualified for the 2015 final.

923. How many returning acts performed in 2015?

924. Which country won the first semi-final in 2015?

925. Which artist won the first semi-final in 2015?
 a   Loïc Nottet
 b   Eduard Romanyuta
 c   Polina Gargarina
 d   Nina Sublatti

926. What was the winning song in the first semi-final in 2015?
 a   'A Million Voices'
 b   'Rhythm Inside'
 c   'Wars for Nothing'
 d   'Autumn Leaves'

927. Which country's 2015 entry became the first non-winning song to gain over 300 points?

928. Georgia and Malta's 2015 entries had the same title. What was it?

929. Artist Trijntje Oosterhuis won the Barbara Dex Award in 2015. Which country did she represent?

930. Which country won the second semi-final in 2015?

931. Which artist won the second semi-final in 2015?
- **a** Monika and Vaidas
- **b** Amber Bondin
- **c** Aminata Savadogo
- **d** Måns Zelmerlöw

932. What was the winning song in the second semi-final in 2015?
- **a** 'Golden Boy'
- **b** 'Heroes'
- **c** 'Love Injected'
- **d** 'Here for You'

933. *RuPaul's Drag Race*, UK, had an episode based around Eurovision. What was the name of the contest in the show?
- **a** *Eurovision Drag Contest*
- **b** *Ruruvision Song Contest*
- **c** *RuPaul's Best Friends Race*
- **d** *Queens of Europe*

934. The 2015 Latvian entry later became Lelle (The Doll) in which popular TV show, syndicated in her home country?

935. Måns Zelmerlöw, Swedish entry in 2015, provided the Russian voice for which Disney character?

936. Name the reality TV show that kick-started the career of 2015 Australian entry Guy Sebastian?

937. Australia was the first country outside the European Broadcasting Area to receive 12 points, in 2015. Which two countries awarded Australia the coveted douze points?

938. Which country won the 2015 final?
    a Austria
    b Australia
    c Germany
    d Sweden

939. Which artist won the 2015 final?
    a Electro Velvet
    b Guy Sebastian
    c Genealogy
    d Måns Zelmerlöw

 **940.** What was the winning song in the 2015 final?

   a 'Heroes'

   b 'One Last Breath'

   c 'A Million Voices'

   d 'Grande Amore' (A Great Love)

941 Which country hosted the 60th anniversary concert, *Eurovision's Greatest Hits*?

942. How many people worldwide tuned into the 60th anniversary concert?

   a 53 million

   b 106 million

   c 197 million

   d 238 million

943. Who presented *Eurovision's Greatest Hits*?

944. Which popular dance act performed in the interval of the anniversary show?

945. Which of these acts did not perform in *Eurovision's Greatest Hits*?

   a Dana International

   b ABBA

   c Conchita Wurst

   d Johnny Logan

946. Who performed for the UK at the 60th Anniversary?

947. Which four songs were included in *Eurovision's Greatest Hits* finale medley?

948. What was the theme of the 2016 contest?
- **a** Come Together
- **b** Let's Have a Sing-Song
- **c** United We Sing
- **d** Ram-a-lam-a-ding-dong

949. True or False: Australia didn't return to Eurovision in 2016, as they had stated they would only return if they won.

950. How many times has Petra Mede hosted Eurovision?

951. Which country qualified for the first time in 2016?

952. Which two countries didn't qualify for the first time in 2016?

953. True or False: No Nordic countries qualified for the final in 2016.

954. What was the title of 2016 presenters Måns Zelmerlöw and Petra Mede's interval number?

955. What did Petra Mede suggest would give a Eurovision number "a contemporary feel" in the 2016 interval number?

956. Besides the presenters' number, which American pop star performed in the 2016 interval act?

957. Which country hasn't missed a single contest since 1959?

958. Which language were all songs translated into in 2016?

959. Which country was forced to pull out of the 2016 contest with only three weeks to spare, due to financial issues?

960. What did the EBU ban from the venue in 2016, sparking controversy?

961. In 2016, the juror from which country got her votes mixed up, resulting in her awarding douze points to the wrong country?

962. Which country won the first semi-final in 2016?
- **a** Malta
- **b** Russia
- **c** Estonia
- **d** Czechia

 963. Which artist won the first semi-final in 2016?
- **a** Iveta Mukuchyan
- **b** Jüri Pootsmann
- **c** Lidia Isac
- **d** Sergey Lazarev

964. What was the winning song in the first semi-final in 2016?
- **a** 'LoveWave'
- **b** 'You Are the Only One'
- **c** 'Utopian Land'
- **d** 'Lighthouse'

965. Who joined 2014 Moldovan entry Lidia Isac on stage during her number?

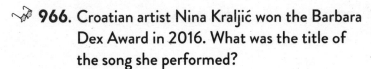

966. Croatian artist Nina Kraljić won the Barbara Dex Award in 2016. What was the title of the song she performed?

a 'Lighthouse'

b 'My House'

c 'Your House'

d 'Glass House'

967. Belarus's 2016 act opened with a hologram of artist IVAN doing what?

968. Which country won the second semi-final in 2016?

969. Which artist won the second semi-final in 2016?

a Jamala

b Kaliopi

c ManuElla

d Dami Im

970. What was the winning song in the second semi-final in 2016?

a '1944'

b 'If Love Was a Crime'

c 'Sound of Silence'

d 'Help You Fly'

971. Where was 2016 Australian entry Dami Im born?

972. Which reality TV series kick-started the career of 2016 Australian entry Dami Im?

973. In 2016, UK entry Joe and Jake competed against one another in which reality TV show?

974. Rumours swirled in 2016 that two countries would join Eurovision for the first time that year. The rumours proved to be untrue but which countries were they?

975. Which country won the 2016 final?
  a Ukraine
  b Belarus
  c Poland
  d Greece

976. Which artist won the 2016 final?
  a Dami Im
  b Jamala
  c Joe and Jake
  d Iveta Mukuchyan

977. What was the winning song in the 2016 final?
- **a** 'Sound of Silence'
- **b** '1944'
- **c** 'Alter Ego'
- **d** 'LoveWave'

978. The 2016 winning number gained criticism for breaking Eurovision's "no politics" rule by criticising which historic political figure?

979. What was the theme of the 2017 contest?
- **a** Celebrate Fame
- **b** Celebrate Luminosity
- **c** Celebrate Diversity
- **d** Celebrate Rhythm

980. Which city hosted the 2017 contest?

981. True or False: 2017 was the first time in three years that both the jury and televote agreed on the winner.

982. The 2017 logo was based on which traditional Ukrainian item?

983. Which of the following was not an official hashtag of the 2017 contest?

a #NulPoints

b #DouzePoints

c #CelebrateDiversity

d #ESC2017

984. Who joined 2007 participant Verka Serduchka to showcase Ukraine in two comedic sketches in the 2017 semi-finals?

985. Which country won the first semi-final in 2017?

a Moldova

b Belgium

c Sweden

d Portugal

986. Which artist won the first semi-final in 2017?

a Salvador Sobral

b Tamara Gachechiladze

c Sunstroke Project

d Norma John

⭐ **987.** What was the title of the winning song in the first semi-final in 2017?

   a 'Hey Mamma'
   b 'City Lights'
   c 'Amar Pelos Dois' (Love for Us Both)
   d 'Keep the Faith'

988. Graham Norton had this to say about the 2017 Italian entry: "If you're going to get someone to dress as a _____, at least get a decent outfit." Fill in the blank.

989. A German website incorrectly claimed in 2017 that Kyiv city workers were doing what?

   a Impounding all taxis without a permit
   b Dressing up as clowns
   c Striking in protest at working conditions
   d Killing street dogs

990. The Head of Delegation for which country resigned in 2017 following a voting scandal in the national final?

991. Which artist's performance was interrupted by a stage invader who flashed their bottom to the camera during the 2017 interval act?

☆ **992.** Which country won the second semi-final?

☆ **993.** Which artist won the second semi-final in 2017?
   a Joci Pápai
   b Kristian Kostov
   c Anja Nissen
   d Brendan Murray

☆ **994.** What was the winning song in the second semi-final in 2017?
   a 'Origo'
   b 'Where I Am'
   c 'Beautiful Mess'
   d 'Rain of Revolution'

🎤 **995.** In 2017, Azerbaijani artist Dihaj performed in front of what at the beginning of her song?

🐁 **996.** Dihaj's performance featured a man standing atop a ladder with what kind of animal head?

🐁 **997.** Artist Slavko Kalezić, winner of the Barbara Dex Award in 2017, represented which country?

🎤 **998.** How old was Bulgarian entry Kristian Kostov when he competed in 2017?

999. Where did UK contestant Lucie Jones finish in the ESC final in 2017?

1000. Which country's entry stole the show with his windmilling ponytail in 2017?

1001. In Netflix documentary show *Travels With My Father*, which former ESC winners do Jack Whitehall and his father meet?

1002. In which Netflix comedy does Benoît tell Mindy that the song he wrote for her has been chosen to represent France in the ESC?

1003. Which country won the 2017 final?
- **a** Austria
- **b** Sweden
- **c** Portugal
- **d** Italy

1004. Which artist won the 2017 final?
- **a** Kristian Kostov
- **b** Salvador Sobral
- **c** Salvador Dali
- **d** Sunstroke Project

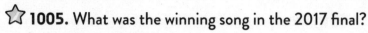

1005. What was the winning song in the 2017 final?

a 'Do It for Your Lover'

b 'Beautiful Mess'

c 'Hey Mamma'

d 'Amar Pelos Dois' (Love for Us Both)

1006. What is the English translation of the Belarusian 2017 song 'Historyja Majho Žyccia'?

a 'Get Me Out of Here'

b 'Story of My Life'

c 'Time for a Story'

d 'History of My Aunt'

1007. How many times have 2017 Moldovian entry Sunstroke Project competed in Eurovision?

1008. What was the theme of Eurovision 2018?

a Swing Time!

b All Aboard!

c Anchors Away!

d Bottoms Up!

1009. How many presenters were there in 2018?

1010. What featured on the 2018 ESC logo?

   a A mermaid

   b The Roman god, Neptune

   c A seashell

   d A wave

1011. Why was the 2018 Eurovision Young Dancers competition cancelled?

   a Nobody was willing to host it

   b Political tensions between the previous year's winner and the current entrants

   c A financial crash in the host nation

   d It was scheduled for April 31st, which doesn't exist

1012. Which country's act was interrupted in 2018 by a stage invader?

1013. Which country won the first semi-final in 2018?

   a Austria

   b France

   c Israel

   d Germany

1014. Which artist won the first semi-final in 2018?

   a   Mikolas Josef

   b   Eleni Foureira

   c   Alekseev

   d   Netta

1015. A contestant from North Macedonia won the Barbara Dex Award in 2018. What was the name of the artist?

   a   Cute Eyes

   b   Hot Lips

   c   Eye Cue

   d   Sweet Face

1016. What did the contestant from North Macedonia wear?

   a   A pink tunic and grey shorts

   b   A ninja costume

   c   A milkmaid's outfit

   d   An emerald green tutu

1017. Which American musician is credited as a songwriter on Israeli singer Netta's 2018 number, 'Toy', due to similarities between the Eurovision hit and one of the musician's songs?

1018. In 2018, which country's artist won their national final by default, after all other competitors either dropped out or were disqualified?

1019. 2018 Swedish artist Benjamin Ingrosso provided his voice for the Swedish dub of which Disney film?

1020. Which country won the second semi-final in 2018?

1021. Which artist won the second semi-final in 2018?
a Benjamin Ingrosso
b Alexander Rybak
c DoReDos
d Christabelle

1022. What was the winning song in the second semi-final in 2018?
a 'My Lucky Day'
b 'Dance You Off'
c 'I Won't Break'
d 'That's How You Write a Song'

1023. What colour was the "red carpet" in the 2018 opening ceremony?

1024. What were the flagbearers dressed as in the 2018 Flag Parade?

1025. Which UK country made its debut in the Junior Eurovision Song Contest in 2018?

1026. Which country has won the Junior Eurovision Song Contest the most times?
- **a** Russia
- **b** Ukraine
- **c** Georgia
- **d** Australia

1027. Popular previous winner Alexander Rybak represented Norway for the second time in 2018. Where did he finish in the grand final?
- **a** First
- **b** Third
- **c** Fifteenth
- **d** Twenty-fourth

1028. Which country's 2018 entry featured Eurovision's first same-sex couple in both their music video and live performance?

☆ **1029.** Which country won the final in 2018?

  a Malta
  b Israel
  c Azerbaijan
  d Greece

☆ **1030.** Which artist won the 2018 Eurovision final?

  a Netta
  b Alexander Rybak
  c Eleni Foureira
  d Benjamin Ingrosso

☆ **1031.** What was the winning song in the 2018 final?

  a 'Fuego' (Fire)
  b 'That's How You Write a Song'
  c 'Toy'
  d 'La Forze' (The Force)

🐾 **1032.** What is the English translation of Hungary's 2018 song, 'Viszlát Nyár'?

  a So Long, Farewell
  b Goodbye Summer
  c Goodbye Winter
  d Hello Spring

1033. Though it was mostly sung in English, Israel's 2018 number, 'Toy', contains the Hebrew lyrics "Ani lo buba". What does this mean?

a "I'm not a doll"
b "I'm not a puppet"
c "Put me on the shelf"
d "Don't play with me"

1034. Besides English and Hebrew, Israel's 2018 number featured which language for the first time in Eurovision history?

1035. What adorned the stage during Netta's performance for Israel in 2018?

1036. What was the theme for the 2019 contest?

a Dare to Dream
b Dare to Live
c Dare to Dance
d I Dare You!

1037. What shape featured on the 2019 logo?

1038. Which city hosted the 2019 contest?

1039. True or False: All four of Israel's Eurovision winners attended the 2019 contest.

1040. Which four previous Eurovision artists performed in the 2019 final's interval song, 'Switch Song'?

1041. True or False: All the performers in 'Switch Song' were previous winners.

1042. Which country won the first semi-final in 2019?

a Georgia
b Belarus
c Australia
d Slovenia

1043. Which artist won the first semi-final in 2019?

a Lake Malawi
b Hatari
c Conan Osíris
d Kate Miller-Heidke

1044. What was the winning song in the first semi-final in 2019?

a 'Look Away'
b 'Zero Gravity'
c 'Friend of a Friend'
d 'Hatrio Mun Sigra' (Hate Will Prevail)

1045. What colour was the "red carpet" in the 2019 opening ceremony?

1046. Which global superstar performed in the interval for the 2019 final?

1047. Which two countries withdrew in 2019?

1048. What were all the artists invited to do in the pre-show postcards in 2019?

1049. Which Portugese artist, with a name that combines a super hero with an Egyptian god, won the Barbara Dex Award in 2019?

1050. Which country won the second semi-final in 2019?
a   Romania
b   Armenia
c   Ireland
d   The Netherlands

1051. Which artist won the second semi-final in 2019?
a   Tamara Todevska
b   John Lundvik
c   Michela
d   Duncan Laurence

1052. What was the winning song in the second semi-final in 2019?

a   'Too Late for Love'

b   'Arcade'

c   'Proud'

d   'That Night'

1053. How does the title of Iceland's dark 2019 song, 'Hatrið Mun Sigra' translate into English?

a   'Hatred Will Prevail'

b   'Til Death Do Us Part'

c   'I'll See You On the Other Side'

d   'One Way Ticket to Hell'

1054. Which of these languages was heard at Eurovision for the first time in 2019 – Abkhaz, Amharic or Swahili?

1055. How often did "na" appear in San Marino's 2019 number, 'Say Na Na Na'?

a   125

b   150

c   175

d   200

1056. Which country's act featured the artist atop a huge pole in 2019?

1057. What did the 2019 Icelandic artist display during the voting section that earned them a €5,000 fine?

1058. True or False: Turkey returned to Eurovision in 2019 for the first time since 2012.

1059. Which country won the 2019 final?
- **a** Iceland
- **b** The Netherlands
- **c** Norway
- **d** Finland

1060. Which artist won the 2019 final?
- **a** Mahmood
- **b** Michael Rice
- **c** Sergey Lazarev
- **d** Duncan Laurence

1061. What was the winning song in the 2019 final?
- **a** 'Bigger Than Us'
- **b** 'Arcade'
- **c** 'Scream'
- **d** 'Soldi' (Money)

🎙 **1062.** Besides English, which language did Norway include in their 2019 number?

🌐 **1063.** A 2019 comedy-thriller featuring a young gay Muslim man trying to represent Israel in Eurovision is named after which iconic Eurovision phrase?

💿 **1064.** Which year's contest was the longest in Eurovision history?

💿 **1065.** How long was the longest grand final in Eurovision history?

🎆 **1066.** In which year was the opening Flag Parade first seen?

🎙 **1067.** In which year was the Green Room first moved into the arena?

🎙 **1068.** What is the maximum number of people allowed on stage per act, including backup dancers?

🎆 **1069.** What song opens every Eurovision Song Contest?

1070. To how many continents is The Eurovision Song Contest broadcast?

1071. Which act holds the record for the greatest number of douze points awarded?

1072. Whose voice did not 'take her there' on the night of Eurovision 2019?

1073. True or False: The Czech Republic has never qualified for a final since semi-finals were introduced.

D **1074.** How many countries have scored nul points on their début?

☆ **1075.** True or False: 2019 saw the eighth consecutive win for a solo performer.

2020 ONWARDS

THE DECADE SO FAR...

• UK LEAVES THE EUROPEAN UNION • COVID-19 BECOMES A GLOBAL PANDEMIC • EVERYONE IS WEARING COMFY PYJAMAS, LOUNGEWEAR AND MASKS • NFTS CHANGE THE WORLD OF CRYPTOCURRENY • HARRY STYLES, BILLIE EILISH AND K-POP SENSATION BTS HIT THE CHARTS • LAUNCH OF JAMES WEBB SPACE TELESCOPE AND THE SEARCH FOR THE EARLY UNIVERSE • *ANIMAL CROSSING* AND *AMONG US* GAMING CRAZES

1076. What was notable about the 2020 Eurovision Song Contest?

1077. Which city was set to host the 2020 contest?

1078. What was the intended theme for the 2020 contest?
  a Open Up
  b Open All Hours
  c Open For Business
  d Open University

1079. What was the 2020 Eurovision venue turned into?

1080. What was the name of the tribute show aired instead of the 2020 contest?

1081. Which previous Eurovision winner inspired the name of the 2020 tribute contest?
  a Lulu
  b Katrina and the Waves
  c Lys Assia
  d Corry Brokken

1082. Which Dutch YouTube personality hosted Eurovisioncalls, where they interviewed each of the 2020 participants?

1083. In what video game did planned 2020 Icelandic entry 'Think About Things' feature?

1084. What is Eurovision Again?

1085. Who created Eurovision Again?

1086. Which of these shows has not been included in Eurovision Again?
- **a** Dublin 1988
- **b** Kyiv 2005
- **c** Brighton 1974
- **d** Stockholm 2000

1087. Who was expected to represent the UK in Eurovision 2020?

1088. What was the intended song for the UK entry in 2020?
- **a** 'My Last Breath'
- **b** 'Space Man'
- **c** 'Embers'
- **d** 'Waterloo But Not That One'

1089. Which country's "lockdown video" of their intended 2020 song went viral on Twitter and TikTok?

1090. Where did Eurovision 2021 take place?

1091. True or False: The 2020 artists were automatically allowed to perform in the 2021 contest.

1092. What is the most streamed Eurovision song of all time?

1093. Which country gained nul points overall in 2021?

1094. Which three countries gained no points from the 2021 televote, only being saved from the dreaded nul points by the juries?

1095. Which of these previous Eurovision winners did not perform in the 2021 interval act?
   a   Lordi
   b   Alexander Rybak
   c   Måns Zelmerlöw
   d   Lenny Kuhr

1096. What "first" did 2021 presenter Nikkie de Jager earn?

1097. What motif was seen in all the pre-show postcards in 2021?

1098. Due to the heightened COVID risk, what were all acts asked to do in advance of the 2021 contest?

1099. Which country had to use its backup recording due to travel restriction?

1100. Which official Eurovision social media account saw each country doing a daily takeover in the lead-up to the 2021 contest?

1101. What was the title of the mini-documentary series included in the 2021 semi-finals, highlighting past winners?

1102. Which country won the first semi-final in 2021?
   a North Macedonia
   b Israel
   c Malta
   d Lithuania

1103. Which artist won the first semi-final in 2021?
   a Go_A
   b Destiny
   c Manizha
   d Elena Tsagrinou

☆ **1104.** What was the winning song in the first semi-final in 2021?

a 'Russian Woman'

b 'Maps'

c 'Shum'

d 'Je Me Casse' (I'm Leaving)

😮 **1105.** Which two countries pulled out of the 2021 live show after their contestants tested positive for COVID-19?

🐭 **1106.** What did German artist Jendrik wear on his opening ceremony outfit in 2021?

💿 **1107.** Which of these languages was heard for the first time in 2021: Azerbaijani, Romani, Sranan Tongo or Georgian?

😮 **1108.** Where is Sranan Tongo spoken and which country featured this language in their song?

🐭 **1109.** Which country's artist dropped their microphone during their performance in 2021?

🐭 **1110.** What was the longest on-stage kiss in Eurovision history?

1111. Which country won the second semi-final in 2021?

   a Finland

   b Bulgaria

   c Iceland

   d Switzerland

 1112. Which artist won the second semi-final in 2021?

   a Gjon's Tears

   b Daoi & Gagnamagnio

   c Victoria

   d Vincent Bueno

 1113. What was the winning song in the second semi-final in 2021?

   a '10 Years'

   b 'Tout L'Univers' (The Whole Universe)

   c 'Last Dance'

   d 'The Moon is Rising'

1114. Tix, Norwegian entrant and winner of the Barbara Dex Award in 2021, wore what?

   a Angel wings

   b Devil horns

   c A zebra striped cloak

   d Comedy sunglasses and moustache

1115. What wardrobe malfunction did 2021 Italian performer Damiano David experience onstage?

1116. How many songs were performed entirely in French in 2021?

1117. Why didn't previous winner Duncan Laurence pass on the trophy to the 2021 winner?

1118. True or False: The top three winners in 2021 were all artists that had been carried over from 2020.

1119. What colour was the "red carpet" in the 2021 and 2022 opening ceremonies?

1120. Which country won the 2021 final?
   a   Italy
   b   North Macedonia
   c   Israel
   d   Ireland

1121. Which artist won the 2021 final?
   a   Måneskin
   b   Gjon's Tears
   c   Barbara Pravi
   d   Trusse

1122. What was the winning song in the 2021 final?

a 'Mata Hari'

b 'Voilà' (Here)

c 'Tout L'Univers' (All the Universe)

d 'Zitti e Buoni' (Shut Up and Be Good)

1123. Which artist holds the record for the highest note reached in a Eurovision contest?

1124. Which two artists did Italian band Måneskin credit as their style icons?

a Mick Jagger and Marianne Faithfull

b David Bowie and Destiny's Child

c Malcolm McLaren and Vivienne Westwood

d George Michael and Mary J Blige

1125. What is the English translation of the Ukrainian song title 'Shum', from 2021?

1126. 2021 UK entry James Newman previously wrote the 2017 Eurovision entry for which country?

1127. Which country's 2021 act drew criticism from Christian groups?

1128. What was the theme of the 2022 contest?
- **a** The Sound of Beauty
- **b** The Art of Noise
- **c** The Beauty of Song
- **d** Song, Beautiful Noise

1129. Which city hosted the 2022 contest?

1130. Which 2022 presenter performed some of their own hits during the final interval?

1131. When was the last time that Norway took last place at Eurovision?

1132. What geological feature was prominently featured in the 2022 stage design?

1133. What was the name of the drone that travelled across Italy for the 2022 pre-show postcards?

1134. Why did 2022 North Macedonian artist Andrea gain criticism from her home country?

1135. Which country won the first semi-final in 2022?

1136. Which artist won the Barbara Dex Award in 2022?

1137. What was the birthplace of Spanish 2022 artist, Chanel?

1138. Which artist won the You're a Vision award in 2022?

1139. Why did the 2022 final only feature 25 participants, rather than the usual 26?

1140. How many songs were sung in French in Eurovision 2022?

1141. Which country won the second semi-final in 2022?
   a   Australia
   b   Serbia
   c   Sweden
   d   Czechia

1142. Which artist won the second semi-final in 2022?

1143. What was the winning song in the second semi-final in 2022?
   a   'Not the Same'
   b   'Lock Me In'
   c   'Stripper'
   d   'Hold Me Closer'

1144. Why was previous winner Måneskin unable to present the Grand Prix to the 2022 winner?

1145. 2022 Australian performer Sheldon Riley became "Snapdragon" in which reality TV show?

1146. 2022 Swedish performer Cornelia Jakobs was a member of which girl group?

1147. Which successful TikTok star represented the UK in the 2022 contest?

1148. Ben Adams, of boy band A1 fame, represented which country in 2022?

1149. Which country won the 2022 final?
   a Ukraine
   b United Kingdom
   c Australia
   d Azerbaijan

1150. Which artist won the 2022 final?
   a Sam Ryder
   b Chanel
   c We Are Domi
   d Kalush Orchestra

1151. What was the winning song in the 2022 final?
- **a** 'Stefania'
- **b** 'Fade to Black'
- **c** 'Space Man'
- **d** 'SloMo'

 1152. In what language was the 2022 winning song sung?

1153. Which of these languages was heard for the first time in 2022 – Latin, Crimean Tatar or Catalan?

1154. What is the name of the nightclub available for Eurovision participants and their delegates?

1155. What are the Marcel Bezençon awards?

1156. What are the three categories in the Marcel Bezençon awards?

1157. How many Eurovision logos have featured a part of the human body?

1158. How many Eurovision logos have featured a bird?

1159. Who is the Poplight Fan Award given to?

1160. As of 2022, which country has the longest qualification streak (not counting the Big Five)?

a Greece
b Portugal
c Ukraine
d Azerbaijan

1161. How many countries awarded UK entry Sam Ryder the highly prized, douze points?

1162. Which European country had the most Eurovision viewers in 2022?

a United Kingdom
b Spain
c Norway
d Germany

1163. In the Apple TV series *Ted Lasso*, what Eurovision event did Roy and Keeley not deem special enough to open a bottle of champagne for?

a Someone's dress catching fire
b Austria singing a song in which the only words were "la la la"
c The UK getting nul points (again)
d Graham Norton being escorted off the premises

1164. As of 2022, which country has the longest non-qualification streak?

   a   Malta

   b   The Netherlands

   c   Bosnia & Herzegovina

   d   San Marino

1165. True or False: No act performing second in the running order has ever won the contest.

1166. Which two countries won the contest in their début year?

1167. What is the name of the titular band in the 2020 Eurovision-inspired film starring Will Ferrell and Rachel McAdams?

1168. What country is at the centre of the 2020 Eurovision film?

1169. In the 2020 Eurovision film, what is the name of the classically Eurovision "nonsense song" that becomes popular in the titular band's home town?

1170. Which country scored the most points in any Eurovision contest?

1171. How many countries that have competed in Eurovision no longer exist?

1172. Which country has only competed in Eurovision once?

🎤 **1173.** As Ukraine is unable to host Eurovision in 2023, which country will take their place?

🎤 **1174.** Which city, home to one of the most iconic bands of the 60s, will play host to the Eurovision Song Contest in 2023?

BEST BURNS

OUCH!

FORGET THE SONGS, FORGET THE POLITICS AND NEVER MIND THE SPECTACLE – WE ALL KNOW WHAT THE EUROVISION SONG CONTEST IS REALLY ABOUT – THE DRAMA! WHETHER IT'S ONE PERFORMER BEING MEAN ABOUT ANOTHER'S COSTUME, A PRESENTER SLIPPING UP AND INSULTING A PARTICULAR COUNTRY'S ACT, OR EVEN A COMMENTATOR DELIVERING A TRULY DEVASTATING ROAST FROM THE BOOTH, THERE'S NOTHING EUROVISION FANS LOVE MORE THAN A GOOD BURN.

IN THIS SECTION, YOU'LL NEED TO CAST YOUR MIND BACK TO SOME OF THE BEST JOKES AND INSULTS FROM EUROVISION HISTORY.

1175. How did UK commentator Terry Wogan describe the unpopularity of the winning song in 1989?

a   "An embarrassment"
b   "Inevitable"
c   "A death knell"
d   "Completely unwarranted"

1176. Complete the Terry Wogan quote: "Every year I expect it to be less _____, and every year it is more so."

a   Embarrassing
b   Political
c   Colourful
d   Foolish

1177. Complete the Terry Wogan quote: "Who knows what hellish future lies ahead? Actually I do, I've seen the _____."

a   Rehearsals
b   Costumes
c   Performers backstage
d   Semi-finals

1178. Complete the quote by Australian commentator Sam Pang: "He walks that fine line between distinguished elder and _____."

a   Grumpy grandpa

b   Drunk uncle

c   Jabba the Hutt

d   Deadbeat dad

1179. Which fictional characters did Terry Wogan compare the 2001 presenters to?

a   Snow White and Darth Vadar

b   The Little Mermaid and Doctor Death

c   Sleeping Beauty and Frankenstein

d   Alice and the Mad Hatter

1180. What did Terry Wogan call 2006 Dutch spokesperson Paul de Leeuw after his shenanigans?

a   An eejit

b   An embarrassment

c   A clown

d   A liability

1181. Complete the Terry Wogan quote: "This has been typified as a Eurosong... they do a little walking and _____".

- **a** Pull out a harp
- **b** Then a costume change
- **c** Bounce a bit
- **d** Don't sing much

1182. Complete the Terry Wogan quote: "They've got four languages in Belgium... and they're singing in _____".

- **a** French
- **b** Greek
- **c** An imaginary one
- **d** None of them

1183. Complete the Graham Norton quote: "In case you're wondering, there hasn't been a_____. She is a fully trained dancer and she's meant to be there."

- **a** Mistake
- **b** Riot
- **c** Stage invader
- **d** Accident

1184. What did Graham Norton compare 2015 Georgian performer Nina Sublatti's costume to?

a   Roadkill

b   Vintage Lady Gaga

c   An angry jackdaw

d   Sid Vicious – the early years

1185. Which 2011 artist did Graham Norton dryly introduce with "there are flashing lights in this performance, but that's not the most disturbing part, as you'll see"?

1186. Which 2013 performance was introduced by commentator Graham Norton's comment, "Small children and pets should probably be moved out of the room"?

1187. Complete the Terry Wogan quote: "I don't know about you, I'm going to ____".

a   Have a stiff drink

b   Resign

c   Lie down in a darkened room

d   Send a robot next year, you'll never tell the difference

1188. Complete the Terry Wogan quote: "It's been a wonderful, wonderful evening. I mean, not musically of course but in terms of _____."

a Brazen political voting
b The drinks
c Sensory overload
d Spectacle

1189. "Answers on a postcard please. Not sure if the man inside was dancing or had just run out of air." To which 2013 performance was commentator Graham Norton referring?

1190. Which country's 2018 performance caused commentator Graham Norton to quip, "You asked for Eurovision, you got Eurovision"?

1191. Complete the Terry Wogan quote: "Hold on. Be strong. Just _____. It'll be over soon."

a Lie back and think of England
b Cling to the wreckage
c Take another sip of whisky
d Don't look directly at it

😆 **1192.** How did 1992 UK entry Michael Ball respond when asked if he'd ever compete in Eurovision again?

a "I'd rather stick needles in my eyes"
b "I don't think they'd take me back"
c "I would love to"
d "Was I in Eurovision? I don't remember"

😆 **1193.** What reason did Graham Norton give for the 2017 Romanian entry's claim that she was the "first yodeller in Romania"?

a Nobody else would want to
b There aren't enough people in Romania
c She hasn't ever left the house
d The others don't talk about it

😆 **1194.** What did Graham Norton compare the 2015 UK entry's costumes to?

a Posh hospital workers from the future
b Bargain basement Cher
c Astronauts who got lost on their way to space
d Terminator meets dental nurse

1195. What did well-known music manager Louis Walsh call the 1998 Irish entry Dawn Martin after she beat one of his bands in the national final?

a   Talentless
b   An amateur
c   A nobody
d   His greatest nemesis

1196. Complete the Sam Pang quote: "That song really broke the spirit in here. And that spirit was _____."

a   Gin
b   Tequila
c   Whisky
d   Vodka

1197. Complete the Graham Norton quote: "He did something terrible as a boy. We don't know what it was. It might have been _____".

a   Murder
b   Selling his soul in exchange for mediocre talent
c   Writing this song
d   Taking the money his mother gave him to buy milk and using it to buy magic beans

1198. What did Terry Wogan say he'd prefer to a backstage skit?

a   Dead silence

b   Going home early

c   Commercials

d   Watching the Ukrainian act again

1199. What 2005 ESC moment prompted Terry Wogan to say "It's not easy, this. You have to move your lips"?

a   The Romanian act forgetting the words

b   The Swedish points announcer struggling to pronounce country names

c   The presenter trying to sing

d   Somebody criticising his commentary style

1200. What did Graham Norton say the 2017 Kyiv arena smelled like?

a   Regret

b   Wet dog

c   Kitty litter tray

d   Desperation

1201. What did Sam Pang say of the 2015 theme, Building Bridges?

a "Anyone crossing that bridge is a braver man than me"

b "Anything to avoid building an actual bridge"

c "Some of these performers might be better suited to bridge building than singing"

d "What does that even mean?"

1202. What reason did Graham Norton give for the introduction of the flag ceremony?

a To add some colour

b To remind everyone which country is which

c To point out how similar the French and Belgian flags are

d To make the ceremony a bit longer

1203. How did commentator Graham Norton describe 2021 Serbian act Hurricane when he said they were "less Destiny's Child, more_____"?

a Bob's your uncle

b Divine resurrected

c Destiny's inappropriate auntie

d Elvis and Madonna's love child

1204. Complete the Terry Wogan quote: "I ____ the Eurovision Song Contest and it will continue long after I'm gone. Just please don't ask me to take it seriously."

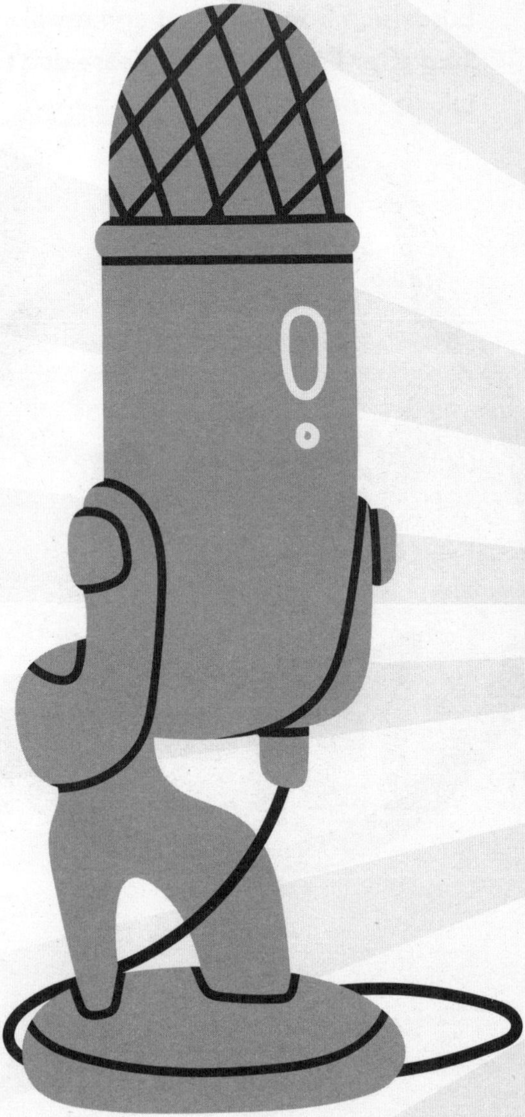

ANSWERS

1956-1959

1. Lugano, Switzerland

2. Switzerland

3. Belgium, France, Germany, Italy, Luxembourg, The Netherlands, Switzerland

4. All seven

5. a) Lys Assia

6. c) 'Refrain'

7. Sanremo Music Festival

8. d) French

9. d) Performers were allowed to vote

10. Two

11. a) Lohengrin Filipello

12. False. Though it was mostly a radio broadcast, some countries broadcast it on TV

13. b) Switzerland

14. 'Das alte Karussell'

15. There is no way of knowing, as the votes were kept secret

16. d) They kissed

17. b) 'Corde Della Mia Chitarra'

18. a) 5 minutes and 9 seconds

19. b) Denmark

20. b) Austria

21. b) Anaïd Iplicjian

22. Two

23. False. This rule hadn't been introduced yet. There was a rumour that Germany was asked to host because they came second, but the 1956 scores were kept secret so no one knows for sure

24. a) 'Que Sera Sera'

25. a) 10

26. The Netherlands

27. a) Corry Brokken

28. d) 'Net Als Toen'

29. True. Voting was secret the previous year

30. One: the UK's 'All'

31. French

32. c) Lawyer

33. b) Bobbejaan Schoepen (Belgium)

34. Sam Payne

35. Flemish

36. Sweden

37. d) France

38. a) Three minutes

39. a) Hannie Lips

40. Two

41. a) Duke Ellington

42. c) Four

43. a) André Claveau

44. b) 'Dors, Mon Amour'

45. No country that has performed second in the running order has ever won the contest

46. a) Three

47. b) They'd done too badly the previous year

48. c) Actress

49. Italian and German

50. Three

51. d) Eyes

52. Domenico Modugno's 'Nel Blu, Dipinto Di Blu' (or 'Volare'), representing Italy

53. The Netherlands

54. b) 16

55. The Netherlands

56. The UK, which hasn't missed a contest since 1958

57. Teddy Scholten

58. b) 'Een Beetje'

59. b) Cannes

60. c) Monaco

61. Luxembourg

62. d) Music experts

63. *Follies*

64. Husband and wife

65. Jacqueline Joubert

66. Windmills

67. Father

68. Alice and Ellen

69. *Playboy*

70. Jean Philippe represented France in 1959 and Switzerland in 1962

THE 60s

71. United Kingdom

72. b) Katie Boyle

73. d) White

74. d) Six

75. a) France

76. c) Jacqueline Boyer

77. a) 'Tom Pillibi'

78. They were brothers

79. c) *The Rudi Carrell Show*

80. German

81. Plagiarism

82. Belgium and Austria

83. a) Luxembourg

84. Jacqueline Joubert

85. a) French

86. c) Jean-Claude Pascal

87. b) 'Nous les Amoureux'

88. c) University of the Arts, Hilversum

89. Spain, Yugoslavia and Finland

90. a) Sweden

91. b) Turkvision Song Contest

92. b) France

93. a) Isabelle Aubret

94. d) 'Un Premier Amour'

95. Four (Spain, Austria, Belgium and The Netherlands)

96. c) Mireille Delannoy

97. Norway

98. d) Denmark

99. Twice

100. a) Katie Boyle

101. b) The Rainbow Alliance

102. d) Israeli

103. c) Oasis

104. a) Grethe and Jørgen Ingmann

105. d) 'Dansevise'

106. Portugal

107. b) Italy

108. d) Gigliola Cinquetti

109. a) 'Non Ho L'Età'

110. Four: Germany, Portugal, Switzerland and Yugoslavia

111. Singer of the Century

112. b) Matt Monro (UK)

113. Bulgarian

114. c) 1991

115. a) Lotte Wæver

116. Nothing, it was empty

117. Twice, in 1963 and 1977

118. a) Female soloists

119. 18

120. Luxembourg

121. a) France Gall

122. 'Poupée de Cire, Poupée de Son'

123. c) Serge Gainsbourg

124. Ireland

125. a) Renata Mauro

126. Four (Belgium, Finland, Germany and Spain)

127. c) 2000

128. Opera

129. a) Ireland

130. Seven

131. Milly Scott in 1966

132. 48 years (they won in 1966 and again in 2014)

133. b) Austria

134. b) Udo Jürgens

135. d) 'Merci, Chérie'

136. a) Josiane Shen

137. Two: Italy and Monaco

138. d) Minister of Culture

139. a) River Clyde

140. French

141. German

142. b) Kenneth McKellar

143. Two: Grethe and Jørgen Ingmann in 1963, and Ell and Nikki in 2011

144. Performing barefoot

145. Two ('1944', Ukraine in 2016 and '22', Ireland in 2019)

146. a) United Kingdom

147. d) Sandie Shaw

148. a) 'Puppet on a String'

149. d) Tom Jones

150. b) Switzerland

151. b) Painter

152. c) Portugal

153. United Kingdom

154. It was the first to be broadcast in colour

155. a) Spain

156. c) Massiel

157. He was replaced because he insisted on singing in Catalan, not Spanish

158. d) 'La, La, La'

159. Cliff Richard

160. c) 'Congratulations'

161. a) Katie Boyle

162. c) Prague

163. Four

164. United Kingdom, France, Spain, The Netherlands

165. c) Six

166. c) Laurita Valenzuela

167. d) Rugby

168. b) Laser therapist

169. "Olé"

170. Scotland

171. Les Misérables, as one of 16 Jean Valjean actors from various countries

172. c) Represent two different countries

173. 1957, at 1 hour and 9 minutes

174. a) Spain

175. c) 'Bonjour, Bonjour'

176. b) Muriel Day

177. Lenny Kuhr, with 'De Troubadour' in 1969

178. c) Him and Her

179. Johnny Logan of Ireland won three times; twice as a performer and once as a songwriter

180. Four

181. Domenico Mudugno's 1958 'Nel Blu Dipinto Di Blu' (or, 'Volare') which has been covered by stars from Dean Martin to David Bowie.

THE 70s

182. 1974

183. a) 1972

184. c) Willy Dobbe

185. False. He is his father

186. Only once

187. a) Coin toss

188. c) Knight

189. Number 2

190. The Netherlands

191. Finland, Norway, Sweden and Portugal all boycotted the contest because they were unhappy about four winners being declared the previous year

192. c) Mary Hopkin

193. b) Ireland

194. a) Dana

195. d) 'All Kinds of Everything'

196. b) Served as a Member of the European Parliament

197. b) Five

198. Each song had to be performed again, and the jury voted on the winner.

199. Malta

200. Group performances of up to six people

201. b) Bernadette Ní Ghallchóir

202. d) She received threats from the IRA.

203. 'Jack-In-The-Box'

204. c) Monaco

205. d) Séverine

206. a) 'Un Banc, Un Arbre, Une Rue'

207. Four (1971, 1976, 1979 and 1981)

208. c) Moira Shearer

209. b) Edinburgh

210. a) Luxembourg

211. a) 6

212. d) Vicky Leandros

213. c) 'Après Toi'

214. b) 'Believe', by Cher

215. d) It was sung in the Irish language

216. Australia

217. d) Yugoslavia and Monaco

218. The Edinburgh Military Tattoo

219. c) Norway

220. Six

221. Get out of their seats

222. d) Helga Guitton

223. b) Luxembourg

224. c) Anne Marie David

225. a) 'Tu Te Reconnaîtras'

226. c) Brats

227. Israel

228. d) Malta

229. It was on the same day as the funeral of their president, Georges Pompidou

230. A referendum on divorce was being held in the country, and there was concern that their song, 'Si', might influence results

231. It was the first signal to launch the Carnation Revolution, which resulted in the overthrow of the Portuguese government

232. Greece

233. d) Katie Boyle

234. *Grease*

235. a) Only artist to finish last more than once

236. b) 60

237. c) Sweden

238. d) ABBA

239. a) 'Waterloo'

240. Napoleon

241. *Mamma Mia!*

242. The Wombles

243. Removed her underwear

244. Turkey

245. They were protesting Turkey's invasion of Cyprus the previous year

246. a) The Netherlands

247. c) Teach-in

248. c) 'Ding-a-Dong'

249. a) Karin Falck

250. The 12, 10, 8-1 points system, still used today

251. They're brothers

252. Corry Brokken, who won the second Eurovision Song Contest in 1957

253. They thought the contest had become too commercial and didn't want to pay to host the contest again

254. c) United Kingdom

255. b) Brotherhood of Man

256. a) 'Save Your Kisses for Me'

257. a) A clown

258. English. There were eight songs sung in English (including Italy's entry, which was sung in both English and Italian)

259. c) 6

260. There was a camera crew strike at the BBC

261. Six: Portugal, Monaco, Austria, Belgium, Israel and Ireland

262. b) Angela Rippon

263. a) Butterflies

264. b) *The Rescuers*

265. d) Spain

266. d) Marie Myriam

267. c) 'L'oiseau et L'enfant'

268. c) Grand pianos

269. b) Frank Naef

270. Colm Wilkinson

271. 20 weeks

272. a) Israel

273. d) Izhar Cohen and Alpha Beta

274. a) 'A-Ba-Ni-Bi'

275. She is the only female conductor to win the contest

276. The Israeli version of *The Masked Singer*

277. True. Denise Fabre and Léon Zitrone presented together

278. False. Lohengrin Filipello presented the inaugural contest in 1956

279. a) Mother's Pride

280. Spain's

281. b) 19

282. It was the first contest to take place outside Europe – in Israel

283. Some countries boycotted the ESC

284. a) Israel

285. a) Gali Atari and Milk and Honey

286. d) 'Hallelujah'

287. b) The most 'la's' in a song

288. Hebrew

289. Genghis Khan

290. 'Agadoo'

291. Brotherhood of Man, 'Save Your Kisses for Me'

292. a) 1970

293. 1978 and 1980

294. True

295. Greece and Cyprus

296. Murder and bank robbery

297. Melbourne, Australia

298. Seven: Germany, The Netherlands, Belgium, Ireland, Luxembourg, Sweden and Switzerland

299. False, though it's a close call: 34 English language songs have won, versus 39 non-English songs

THE 80s

300. The Hague

301. *Songs of Europe*

302. a) It was a fundraiser for the International Red Cross

303. d) 29

304. b) Four

305. Once

306. c) Ireland

307. d) Johnny Logan

308. c) 'What's Another Year?'

309. Penguins

310. Using a different telephone for each country

311. Germany's Katja Ebstein

312. Belgium's

313. "I don't have it."

314. Luxembourg

315. a) United Kingdom

316. c) Bucks Fizz

317. 'Making Your Mind Up'

318. Norway

319. The men removed the women's skirts, to reveal mini-skirts beneath

320. b) A car accident

321. Original Bucks Fizz

322. c) Doctor

323. France

324. "Where is Harrogate?"

325. a) Jan Leeming

326. c) France

327. a) Nicole

328. c) 'Ein Bisschen Frieden'

329. Two: Merci, Chérie in 1966, and Ein Bisschen Frieden in 1982

330. Due to strike action at RTE, their main broadcaster

331. d) Luxembourg

332. c) Corinne Hermès

333. b) 'Si La Vie est Cadeau'

334. Two: Spain and Turkey

335. *Pop Idol*

336. *Double Trouble*

337. They're brothers

338. *The Prince of Egypt*

339. 19

340. Four: English, French, German and Luxembourgish

341. United Kingdom

342. b) Sweden

343. a) Herreys

344. a) 'Diggiloo Diggiley'

345. Heathrow Airport, London, UK

346. Clean-cut Swedish act, The Herreys

347. Lill Lindfors

348. A staged 'wardrobe malfunction' where the skirt of her dress was ripped off, only to reveal a full-length gown

349. Second

350. True

351. c) Norway

352. d) Bobbysocks!

353. d) 'La Det Swinge'

354. Two

355. Rap

356. a) The only band to finish second twice

357. Because Norway had come last so many times

358. Terry Wogan

359. It wasn't performed, as Yugoslavia pulled out of the event

360. Yugoslavia and the Netherlands

361. Iceland

362. a) Luxembourg

363. *Titanic*

364. Sandra Kim, who won for Belgium in 1986, aged 13

365. Åse Kleveland

366. c) Belgium

367. b) Sandra Kim

368. 'J'aime La Vie'

369. United Kingdom

370. Once, in 1986

371. Ireland's Johnny Logan

372. d) Ten

373. a) Ireland

374. c) Johnny Logan

375. 'Hold Me Now'

376. Alongside other Belgian cartoonists, he designed the postcards introducing every country

377. The Brussels Dance Conservatory

378. d) Viktor Lazlo

379. Turkey

380. The Blues Brothers

381. c) Dublin, Ireland

382. Because they submitted a song that they had previously performed

383. Johnny Logan reprising his 1987 winning song, 'Hold Me Now'

384. d) Switzerland

385. a) Celine Dion

386. c) 'Ne Partez Pas Sans Moi'

387. One

388. Canada

389. 12

390. c) Number 3

391. 'Ne Partez Pas Sans Moi' by Celine Dion, winner in 1988

392. *Father Ted*

393. *The Hunchback of Notre Dame*

394. True

395. If two countries are tied, the song with the most 12-point scores wins

396. Iceland

397. Twice

398. 12

399. Organisation Générale des Amateurs de l'Eurovision (General Organisation of Eurovision Fans)

400. 1984

401. c) Yugoslavia

402. Croatian

403. a) Riva

404. 'Rock Me'

405. They didn't confirm their attendance until after the deadline

406. Lausanne, Switzerland

407. a) UEFA Euro Cup

408. Every time the European Broadcasting Union announces a list of 43 participating countries, an incident leads to at least one country withdrawing

409. Four (2009, 2012, 2016 and 2017)

410. 25

411. True. Four were French and one was Greek

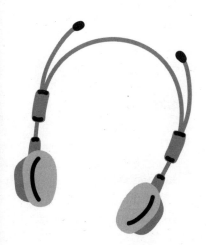

THE 90s

412. False

413. Fall of the Berlin Wall

414. *Zagreb: City of Music*

415. They were so high that tickets were sold on the black market

416. They found out that they may be replaced by younger presenters, and publicly resigned

417. 16

418. Eurocat

419. France, Germany, Italy, Spain, United Kingdom

420. They are automatically entered into the finals, regardless of placing the previous year

421. France

422. Three: France, Germany and Italy

423. b) Italy

424. c) Toto Cutugno

425. 'Insieme: 1992'

426. Their backing track failed to start

427. Two

428. The Gulf War

429. c) Sweden and France

430. Sweden

431. Austria

432. Guitar

433. c) Saxophone

434. c) Italian

435. a) Perfecting their look

436. Husband and wife

437. *Eastenders*

438. d) Carola

439. 'Fångad av en Stormvind'

440. Malmö, Sweden

441. Yugoslavia

442. Eurobird

443. d) Ireland

444. b) Linda Martin

445. a) 'Why Me?'

446. b) A nun

447. Johnny Logan

448. a) *Wicked*

449. Falling off her chair

450. b) Economics

451. Accordion

452. a) Fionnuala Sweeney

453. Millstreet, Ireland, in 1993

454. Croatia, Slovenia and Bosnia and Herzegovina

455. The lowest-placing six countries would not be allowed to enter the following year's contest

456. Malta

457. Linda Martin and Johnny Logan

458. Cyprus

459. c) Ireland

460. c) Niamh Kavanagh

461. 'In Your Eyes'

462. Four: Ireland, Spain, Luxembourg and Israel

463. False: Ireland has reached the Top 5 18 times.

464. False. At 187, it was the highest winning score so far

465. True

466. Ireland and the UK

467. c) Eochaid and Étain

468. Belgium

469. Seven: Estonia, Lithuania, Russia, Poland, Romania, Hungary and Slovakia

470. Just one: Ireland, in 1992, 1993 and 1994

471. Riverdance

472. c) Jean Butler and Michael Flatley

473. a) Ireland

474. a) Paul Harrington and Charlie McGettigan

475. 'Rock 'n' Roll Kids'

476. Belgium

477. *Riverdance*, the interval act

478. b) English

479. Lithuania

480. b) Mary Kennedy

481. *Father Ted* (*A Song for Europe*)

482. False. This occurred again in 2021

483. Germany

484. Johnny Logan

485. c) Norway

486. d) Secret Garden

487. a) 'Nocturne'

488. b) 'You Raise Me Up'

489. A-ha

490. Gina G

491. b) *Derry Girls*

492. d) Yoga

493. *The Masked Singer*, UK

494. False. It was introduced for the first time in 1997

495. Gina G, with 'Ooh Aah, Just a Little Bit'

496. North Macedonia

497. None

498. Seven: Denmark, North Macedonia, Germany, Hungary, Israel, Romania and Russia

499. Sweden

500. a) One More Time

501. 'Den Vilda'

502. a) Ireland

503. c) Eimear Quinn

504. 'The Voice'

505. The minimum age limit; she wouldn't turn 16 for another eight months

506. a) Breton

507. Queen Elizabeth II

508. b) *Love Actually*

509. True. From 1997, instruments on stage became optional

510. Christine Marchal-Oritz

511. Euro Song 1996

512. Eighth

513. Boyzone

514. 'Walking on Sunshine'

515. USA

516. c) *James Bond*

517. United Kingdom

518. False. The previous year's pre-qualifier was unpopular and was replaced with a new system, where countries with the lowest average score over four years would be relegated

519. Five: Austria, Switzerland, United Kingdom, Sweden and Germany

520. It was on their National Holocaust Remembrance Day

521. Bosnia and Herzegovina

522. a) You're a Vision award

523. House of Eurovision

524. Malta's Debbie Scerri

525. Norway and Portugal

526. Ireland, Austria, Germany and Croatia

527. c) United Kingdom

528. Love Shine a Light

529. The Samaritans

530. An animal shelter

531. c) Edith Piaf

532. b) First openly gay performer

533. Ireland

534. Sweden

535. c) Birmingham

536. Switzerland

537. Climbing the scaffolding on stage

538. They awarded Germany zero points instead of the intended 12

539. Responding to Dutch presenter Conny Vandenbos, who said she had previously performed in Eurovision, Ulrika asked, "Long time ago, was it?".

540. True

541. b) Israel

542. d) Dana International

543. b) 'Diva'

544. Celine Dion

545. Parrot feathers

546. c) *Cars*

547. Dana International, in 1998

548. False. There were three presenters in 1999

549. The Balkan War

550. Symbols of the Zodiac

551. She used electronic backing vocals

552. 'No Quiero Eschuchar', by Lydia for Spain

553. c) Sweden

554. d) Charlotte Nilsson

555. b) 'Take Me to Your Heaven'

556. Lydia, representing Spain

557. Jerusalem

558. a) North Macedonia

559. Twice, in 1999 and 2008

560. False. Both Izhar Cohen and Gali Ateri from Milk and Honey attended as guests of honour

561. That songs had to be sung (at least partially) in the act's native language.

562. Norway's 1995 entry, 'Nocturne', which contained only 25 words.

563. They perform the entries in rehearsals, to assist the technical team.

564. ABBA. Their 1992 album Gold spent 828 weeks in the top 100

565. 1996

566. False. Live animals are banned from ESC

567. Five: Sandie Shaw (1967), Sertab Erener (2003), Dima Bilan (2008), Loreen (2012) and Emmelie De Forest (2013)

THE 00s

568. d) Latvia

569. Lips

570. c) Excellent Swedish Design award

571. An official CD

572. Canada, USA and Japan

573. Once Upon a Time, Europe Was Covered with Ice

574. Israel

575. a) "Good Evening Europe!"

576. False. Though some called for a disqualification, the EBU rejected this.

577. c) Denmark

578. a) Olsen Brothers

579. d) 'Fly on the Wings of Love'

580. True. British bookmakers offered 150-1 odds of their victory

581. Belgium's Nathalie Sorce

582. Flying Syrian flags

583. 12

584. 36 years

585. False. With over 38,000 people attending, Parken Stadium was the biggest venue to date

586. Natasja Crone Back and Søren Pilmark

587. b) The youngest winner in Eurovision history

588. Three: Belgium (2003 and 2008) and the Netherlands (2006)

589. True. They performed their winning song, 'Fly on the Wings of Love', alongside their new single, 'Walk Right Back'

590. Piasek

591. c) Estonia

592. d) Tanel Padar, Dave Benton & 2XL

593. a) 'Everybody'

594. False. Denmark came in second in 2002

595. Portugal

596. Latvia

597. Modern Fairytale

598. c) 'A Little Story in the Music'

599. 100% televote

600. There were allegations of jury cheating between certain countries

601. Michalis Rakintzis

602. Ireland and Norway

603. Latvia

604. b) Marie N

605. Pink

606. a) 'I Wanna'

607. Estonia and United Kingdom

608. Four: entries from Slovenia, France, Switzerland and North Macedonia

609. False. It didn't sell well, even in Latvia

610. United Kingdom

611. They couldn't hear the backing track

612. Ukraine

613. 26

614. Riga

615. b) Magical Rendez-vous

616. c) All rivers flow toward the sea, all songs flow toward the Eurovision Song Contest

617. The Iraq War

618. b) UK

619. The UK's 2003 entry, 'Cry Baby'

620. True. The last time all representatives were new to the contest was 1989

621. b) Turkey

622. a) Sertab Erener

623. b) 'Everyway That I Can'

624. Russia's t.A.T.u.

625. Russia

626. Belgium

627. False. There were only three points between first and third place

628. d) Under the Same Sky

629. Albania, Andorra, Belarus and Serbia and Montenegro

630. A semi-final round

631. Twice, Switzerland in 2004 and the Czech Republic in 2009

632. Armenia, Kosovo, Puerto Rico and Australia

633. A DVD of the event

634. d) Switzerland

635. None

636. France, Poland and Russia

637. d) Serbia and Montenegro

638. c) Željko Joksimović

639. a) 'Lane Moje'

640. Catalan, Ukrainian, Latvian and Võro

641. Sanda Ladosi

642. d) Ukraine

643. False. It was Ukraine's second time

644. d) Ruslana

645. c) 'Wild Dances'

646. ABBA's

647. Moldova and Bulgaria

648. "Nul Points"

649. Katie Price, aka Jordan

650. Julio Iglesias, who represented Spain in 1970

651. a) Awakening

652. False

653. Andorra and Monaco

654. A minimum threshold was introduced for televotes, otherwise they would be replaced by a jury

655. Romania

656. d) Luminita Anghel and Sistem

657. a) 'Let Me Try'

658. Austria

659. b) Greece

660. d) Helena Paparizou

661. b) 'My Number One'

662. True

663. Denmark

664. 'Congratulations', sung by Cliff Richard, for the UK, in 1968

665. b) 2.5 million

666. Katrina Leskanich and Renārs Kaupers

667. 14

668. 'Waterloo' by ABBA

669. d) 'Congratulations' by Cliff Richard

670. Ireland

671. Boyzone

672. To save time

673. Maria Menounos and Sakis Rouvas

674. c) The Phaistos Disc

675. d) Feel the Rhythm

676. His phone number

677. Armenia

678. Serbia and Montenegro

679. Ireland

680. Finland

681. b) Lordi

682. 'Hard Rock Hallelujah'

683. One

684. The winners

685. Portugal

686. a) Finland

687. Monster masks

688. 'The Ketchup Song'

689. a) True Fantasy

690. 42

691. The Czech Republic, Georgia, Montenegro and Serbia

692. Monaco

693. Santa Claus

694. Some countries were allowed to choose their position in the running order (five for the semi-final and three for the final)

695. False. They all chose spots in the second half

696. Serbia

697. b) Marija Šerifović

698. c) 'Molitva'

699. Vivienne Westwood

700. Russian, English, Ukrainian and German

701. Whipped cream

702. d) A star

703. *Spy*

704. Silver

705. A vampire

706. Flight attendants

707. c) Serbia

708. a) Marija Šerifović

709. a) 'Molitva'

710. Serbian

711. Helsinki

712. The Beauty Queens

713. As a protest against political voting

714. Three; two semi-finals and one final

715. Sing in French

716. c) A golf buggy

717. c) Confluence of Sound

718. 'Video Killed the Radio Star'

719. San Marino and Azerbaijan

720. The Big Four: Germany, Spain, France and UK, and the host country, Serbia

721. c) Greece

722. d) Kalomira

723. b) 'Secret Combination'

724. Pirates

725. He inhaled helium from a balloon

726. A glass microphone

727. A toy guitar

728. c) Ukraine

729. a) Ani Lorak

730. c) 'Shady Lady'

731. Dustin the Turkey

732. *Riverdance*

733. a) A bronze and silver metallic tutu

734. 2005

735. Onions

736. Elsa from *Frozen*

737. As an angel and a devil

738. c) A washing basket

739. Ukraine's

740. b) Russia

741. d) Dima Bilan

742. a) 'Believe'

743. b) Prince Hans in *Frozen*

744. 2006

745. Due to political content in their song

746. Greta Thunberg

747. a) Firebird

748. Australia

749. Terry Wogan

750. Graham Norton

751. The Czech Republic

752. Iceland

753. d) Yohanna

754. d) 'Is It True?'

755. A scheduling error leading to it being aired late

756. b) Norway

757. b) Alexander Rybak

758. Dita von Teese

759. d) Green jeans

760. Violin/fiddle

761. Belarus

762. True. It debuted at Number 10. Previously, Ireland's Johnny Logan reached Number 2 in 1987

763. A technical error with the telephone operator

764. a) Norway

765. a) Alexander Rybak

766. d) 'Fairytale'

767. c) Andrew Lloyd Webber

768. *Your Country Needs You*

769. 18

770. c) Roman soldiers

771. *Fairytales*

772. 2004

773. c) Portugal

774. 53 years

775. Dave Benton, who won for Estonia in 2001 aged 50 years and 4 months

776. English, though she is played by a Swedish actress

777. b) Olimpiysky Arena

778. Amsterdam, the Netherlands

779. a) Lordi, singing 'Hard Rock Hallelujah' in Helsinki's Market Square

780. 2003

781. c) Olympic Indoor Arena

782. b) Estonia, Finland and Germany

783. 9–14 years

784. c) The performer's language

THE 10s

785. The Czech Republic, Hungary, Montenegro and Andorra

786. a) Share the Moment

787. c) Belgium

788. a) Tom Dice

789. d) 'Me and My Guitar'

790. He won the Barbara Dex Award

791. False. It was the first time that Sweden didn't qualify

792. The 2010 FIFA World Cup

793. a) Turkey

794. b) MaNga

795. a) 'We Could Be the Same'

796. Pink

797. Saxophone

798. Butterflies

799. 22nd

800. c) Germany

801. d) Lena Meyer-Landrut

802. a) 'Satellite'

803. Transparent pianos

804. Four

805. c) Feel Your Heart Beat

806. Dusseldorf

807. False. It was the first

808. Italy

809. Anke Engelke, Judith Rakers and Stefan Raab

810. A heart gesture

811. True. She came 10th

812. b) Greece

813. c) Loukas Giorkas ft. Stereo Mike

814. b) 'Watch My Dance'

815. Georgia

816. When an artist wears green or uses it on stage, they often do badly (or win the Barbara Dex award)

817. Germany's Katja Ebstein in 1970

818. Unicycle

819. a) Sweden

820. d) Eric Saade

821. d) 'Popular'

822. Second

823. False. No songs were sung in French in 2011, aside from a couple of lines in the Lithuanian entry

824. d) Azerbaijan

825. a) Ell and Nikki

826. a) 'Running Scared'

827. *The X Factor*

828. Twin brothers

829. 'Lipstick'

830. True. They entered their national selection competition as solo performers and became a duo when they tied for first place

831. a) Light your fire!

832. Eldar Gasimov, who was one half of the 2011 winning act

833. c) Russia

834. c) Buranovskiye Babushki

835. d) 'Party for Everybody'

836. b) 9

837. Due to a recent catastrophic bus crash, they decided it would be in poor taste

838. All three

839. Four: Jónsi, Jedward, Kaliopi and Željko Joksimović

840. d) Sweden

841. a) Loreen

842. d) 'Euphoria'

843. The UEFA European Football Championship

844. c) A dreadlock

845. d) Liechtenstein

846. Engelbert Humperdinck

847. b) Bake bread

848. b) Sweden

849. c) Loreen

850. d) 'Euphoria'

851. Switzerland's Emil Ramsauer (94)

852. c) We Are One

853. A butterfly

854. d) A wedding dress

855. Malmö

856. c) Wind machine

857. Number 1

858. Free alcohol

859. Petra Mede

860. c) *Cupcakes*

861. False. She was the first solo presenter in 18 years

862. They claimed it was unfair that the Big Five auto-qualify for the final

863. b) One

864. It was accompanied by many people using sign language

865. b) Denmark

866. b) It lit up in flames

867. Eleven

868. 57

869. 1993

870. Beige

871. *The First Voice of Serbia*

872. d) Azerbaijan

873. c) Farid Mammadov

874. 39

875. Astronauts and a cyborg

876. c) Bonnie Tyler

877. c) Wales

878. 1992

879. b) Denmark

880. a) Emmelie de Forest

881. a) 'Only Teardrops'

882. Cascada

883. 21st

884. Northern Ireland

885. Ireland

886. b) #JoinUs

887. They performed in the second semi-final interval act

888. A diamond

889. Their country's flag

890. Lise Rønne, Nikolaj Koppel and Pilou Askæk

891. 12, in the 'Twelve Point Song'

892. c) ABBA

893. Austria's 1976 entry, Waterloo & Robinson

894. Croatia's 1996 entry, Sveta ljubav

895. Three: 2012, 2013 and 2014

896. The Netherlands

897. d) The Common Linnets

898. b) 'Calm After the Storm'

899. "We Are Slavic"

900. Lithuania

901. a) Black and blue

902. SF1: 16, SF2: 15

903. 69 (there were 4 winners in 1969)

904. b) Sausage

905. My World

906. False. They took 17th place, while France came last

907. A hamster wheel

908. b) Gold

909. d) Austria

910. a) Conchita Wurst

911. c) 'Rise Like a Phoenix'

912. False. The record was set the following year, in 2015

913. 27

914. Six: in 2001, 2003, 2005, 2007, 2008 and 2011

915. Thomas Neuwirth

916. d) "It's all the same to me"

917. c) Building Bridges

918. Australia

919. Austria and Germany

920. Sweden and Azerbaijan

921. Booing

922. True

923. Eight

924. Russia

925. c) Polina Gargarina

926. a) 'A Million Voices'

927. Russia's

928. 'Warrior'

929. The Netherlands

930. Sweden

931. d) Måns Zelmerlöw

932. b) 'Heroes'

933. b) *Ruruvision Song Contest*

934. *The Masked Singer* (in Latvia)

935. Flynn Rider in *Tangled*

936. *Australian Idol*

937. Sweden and Austria

938. d) Sweden

939. d) Måns Zelmerlöw

940. a) 'Heroes'

941. United Kingdom

942. c) 197 million

943. Graham Norton and Petra Mede

944. *Riverdance*

945. b) ABBA

946. Brotherhood of Man

947. 'Hallelujah, 'Nel Blu Dipinto Di Blu', 'Making Your Mind Up' and 'Bobbysocks!'

948. d) Come Together

949. False. They did initially say they wouldn't return if they lost, but they decided to compete anyway

950. Two (three including the 60th anniversary concert)

951. The Czech Republic

952. Greece and Bosnia and Herzegovina

953. True

954. 'Love Love Peace Peace'

955. A DJ

956. Justin Timberlake

957. United Kingdom

958. Sign language

959. Romania

960. Regional flags

961. Denmark

962. b) Russia

963. d) Sergey Lazarev

964. b) 'You Are the Only One'

965. A male dancer dressed as an astronaut

966. a) 'Lighthouse'

967. Howling alongside a wolf while naked

968. Australia

969. d) Dami Im

970. c) 'Sound of Silence'

971. South Korea

972. *The X Factor*, Australia

973. *The Voice*, UK

974. China and Kosovo

975. a) Ukraine

976. b) Jamala

977. b) '1944'

978. Josef Stalin

979. c) Celebrate Diversity

980. Kyiv, Ukraine

981. True. The last time was in 2014

982. Namysto, a wooden beaded necklace

983. a) #NulPoints

984. Their mother

985. d) Portugal

986. a) Salvador Sobral

987. c) 'Amar Pelos Dois'

988. Gorilla

989. d) Killing street dogs

990. Spain

991. Jamala

992. Bulgaria

993. b) Kristian Kostov

994. c) 'Beautiful Mess'

995. A blackboard

996. a) Horse head

997. Montenegro

998. 17

999. 15th

1000. Montenegro's

1001. Sunstroke Project (2010)

1002. *Emily in Paris*

1003. c) Portugal

1004. b) Salvador Sobral

1005. d) 'Amar Pelos Dois'

1006. b) 'Story of My Life'

1007. Twice, in 2010 and 2017

1008. b) All Aboard!

1009. Four

1010. c) A seashell

1011. a) Nobody was willing to host it

1012. United Kingdom's

1013. c) Israel

1014. d) Netta

1015. c) Eye Cue

1016. a) A pink tunic and grey shorts

1017. Jack White (of the White Stripes)

1018. Greece's Eleni Foureira

1019. *Big Hero 6*

1020. Norway

1021. b) Alexander Rybak

1022. d) 'That's How You Write a Song'

1023. Blue

1024. Sailors

1025. Wales

1026. c) Georgia

1027. c) Fifteenth

1028. Ireland's

1029. b) Israel

1030. a) Netta

1031. c) 'Toy'

1032. b) 'Goodbye Summer'

1033. a) "I'm not a doll"

1034. Japanese

1035. Lucky cats

1036. a) Dare to Dream

1037. A star

1038. Tel Aviv, Israel

1039. True. Gali Atari, Dana International and Netta performed, and Izhar Cohen was the jury spokesperson

1040. Conchita Wurst, Måns Zelmerlöw, Eleni Foureira and Verka Serduchka

1041. False. Eleni Foureira and Verka Serduchka both came second in their respective years

1042. c) Australia

1043. d) Kate Miller-Heidke

1044. b) 'Zero Gravity'

1045. Orange

1046. Madonna

1047. Bulgaria & Ukraine

1048. Dance

1049. Conan Osíris

1050. d) The Netherlands

1051. d) Duncan Laurence

1052. b) 'Arcade'

1053. a) 'Hatred Will Prevail'

1054. Abkhaz and Amharic

1055. a) 125

1056. Australia's

1057. Palestinian flag scarves

1058. False. They claimed that Israel's win the previous year was pre-planned, and refused to enter the contest

1059. b) The Netherlands

1060. d) Duncan Laurence

1061. b) 'Arcade'

1062. Northern Sami

1063. Douze points

1064. 2019

1065. 4 hours and 11 mins

1066. 2013

1067. 2012

1068. Six

1069. 'Prélude du Te Deum' by Marc-Antoine Charpentier

1070. Five

1071. Sweden's 2012 entry, 'Euphoria' by Loreen, which received top marks from 18 different countries

1072. Madonna failed to reach some of the high notes in 'Like a Prayer'

1073. False. They qualified for the first time in 2016, leaving Andorra as the only country never to qualify

1074. Two: Portugal and Lithuania

1075. True. This was broken in 2021 (with 2020's contest being cancelled)

2020 ONWARDS

1076. It was cancelled due to the COVID-19 pandemic

1077. Rotterdam, The Netherlands

1078. a) Open Up

ANSWERS

1079. A temporary COVID hospital

1080. *Europe Shine a Light*

1081. b) Katrina and the Waves

1082. NikkieTutorials

1083. *Just Dance 2022*

1084. An interactive viewing party of past Eurovision contests, hosted on Twitter

1085. British journalist Rob Holley

1086. d) Stockholm 2000

1087. James Newman

1088. a) 'My Last Breath'

1089. Iceland's Dadi & Gagnamagnio

1090. Rotterdam, The Netherlands

1091. False, though 26 of the 2020 artists did return

1092. 'Arcade' by Duncan Laurence (The Netherlands' 2019 entry)

1093. United Kingdom

1094. Germany, Spain and The Netherlands

1095. b) Alexander Rybak

1096. She was the first transgender host in Eurovision history

1097. Tiny houses

1098. Record a "live-on-tape" recording to use as backup in the event that they couldn't attend the contest

1099. Australia

1100. Instagram

1101. *A Winner's Journey*

1102. c) Malta

1103. b) Destiny

1104. 'Je Me Casse'

1105. Iceland and Poland

1106. Badges containing the photos of the participants unable to attend the ceremony due to COVID

1107. Azerbaijani and Sranan Tongo

1108. Sranan Tongo is spoken in Surinam and the language featured in the song from The Netherlands.

1109. Moldova's

1110. Birth Wilke and Gustav Winckler, in 1957

1111. d) Switzerland

1112. a) Gjon's Tears

1113. b) 'Tout L'Univers'

1114. a) Angel wings

1115. His trouser leg ripped open

1116. Two: France and Switzerland's entries

1117. He tested positive for COVID-19

1118. False. Only one did, as Gjon's Tears made it to third place

1119. Turquoise

1120. a) Italy

1121. a) Måneskin

1122. d) 'Zitti e Buoni'

1123. Israel's 2021 entry, Eden Alene

1124. b) David Bowie and Destiny's Child

1125. Noise

1126. Ireland

1127. Cyprus's act, El Diablo (which translates as The Devil)

1128. a) The Sound of Beauty

1129. Turin, Italy

1130. Mika

1131. 2001

1132. The waterfall

1133. Leo

1134. She threw a flag on the ground

1135. Ukraine

1136. No one: the award was cancelled

1137. Cuba

1138. Australia's Sheldon Riley

1139. The host was a Big Five country, so already auto-qualified

1140. None

1141. c) Sweden

1142. Cornelia Jakobs

1143. d) 'Hold Me Closer'

1144. Frontman Damiano David had injured his leg

1145. *The Masked Singer*, Australia

1146. Love Generation

1147. Sam Ryder

1148. Norway

1149. a) Ukraine

1150. d) Kalush Orchestra

1151. a) 'Stefania'

1152. Ukrainian

1153. Latin

1154. EuroClub

1155. An award named after the late broadcaster who founded the contest, rewarding the best competing songs in the grand final

1156. Press award, Artistic award, Composer award

1157. Three: eyes in 1958, and lips in 1990 and 2000

1158. Two: 1974 and 2009

1159. Best performer under the age of 25

1160. c) Ukraine

1161. Nine

1162. a) United Kingdom

1163. c) The UK getting nul points (again)

1164. b) The Netherlands

1165. True

1166. Switzerland (1956) and Serbia (2007)

1167. Fire Saga

1168. Iceland

1169. 'Ja Ja Ding Dong'

1170. Portugal, whose 2017 entry Salvador Sobral gained 758 points

1171. Two: Yugoslavia broke up in 1992, and Serbia and Montenegro broke up in 2006

1172. Morocco, which competed in 1980

1173. United Kingdom

1174. Liverpool

BEST BURNS

1175. c) " A death knell"

1176. d) Foolish

1177. a) Rehearsals

1178. b) Drunk uncle

1179. b) The Little Mermaid and Doctor Death

1180. a) An eejit

1181. c) Bounce a bit

1182. c) An imaginary one

1183. c) Stage invader

1184. a) Roadkill

1185. Moldova's Zdob si Zdub

1186. Romania's Cezar, 'It's My Life'

1187. a) Have a stiff drink

1188. d) Spectacle

1189. Azerbaijan's Farid Mammadov, 'Hold Me'

1190. Ukraine's act, Mélovin

1191. b) Cling to the wreckage

1192. a) I'd rather stick needles in my eyes

1193. d) The others don't talk about it

1194. a) Posh hospital workers from the future

1195. b) An amateur

1196. d) Vodka

1197. c) Writing this song

1198. c) Commercials

1199. b) The Swedish points announcer struggling to pronounce country names

1200. b) Wet dog

1201. b) Anything to avoid building an actual bridge

1202. d) To make the ceremony a bit longer

1203. c) Destiny's inappropriate auntie

1204. Love